Praise for *Manning Up*

"Kay Hymowitz does an exacting job describing the growing flock of man/children we're seeing, and she lays out the disturbing reality of the 'marriageable mate' dilemma that once affected only black women but has now become a broader phenomenon. Not only are there fewer college-educated men to marry, but many of those men who are available are little more than man/children—not anyone you would want your daughters to marry!"

    —Richard Whitmire, author of *Why Boys Fail*

"If you're curious as to why university admissions officers have to scramble these days to keep their entering classes at less than 60 percent female, or if you find that a sports bar on a Saturday afternoon sounds like a high school locker room, Kay Hymowitz's *Manning Up* provides an illuminating response. It's not because feminism has emasculated men, or because the media parade one man-boy after another (Adam Sandler, Will Ferrell, *The Man Show* . . .). It's because of the knowledge economy. Manhood used to happen through marriage and fatherhood, boys becoming men by assuming caretaking responsibilities, usually by taking jobs in manufacturing. It *made* them grow up. The knowledge economy delays the process. It keeps them longer in school, and many of the jobs it offers favor women (design, communications). Drawing evocatively from films and novels, video games, blogs and research reports, female despair and male slackerdom, Hymowitz derives a fresh and pointed take on the Mars-and-Venus gender gap. This is the startling and persuasive news she imparts, an unintended consequence of the knowledge boom. More prosperity and innovation and media—but at a profound cost to family and society: the immaturity of men."

    —Mark Bauerlein, author of *The Dumbest Generation*

MANNING UP

How the RISE OF WOMEN
Has Turned MEN into BOYS

KAY S. HYMOWITZ

CITY

A City Journal Book

BASIC BOOKS
A Member of the Perseus Books Group
New York

Published by Basic Books,
A Member of the Perseus Books Group

Books published by Basic Books are available at special discounts for bulk purchases
in the United States by corporations, institutions, and other organizations. For
more information, please contact the Special Markets Department at the Perseus
Books Group, 2300 Chestnut Street, Suite 200, Philadelphia, PA 19103, or call
(800) 810-4145, ext. 5000, or e-mail special.markets@perseusbooks.com.

Designed by Trish Wilkinson
Set in 11 point Goudy Old Style

Library of Congress Cataloging-in-Publication Data

Hymowitz, Kay S., 1948–
    Manning up : how the rise of women has turned men into boys / Kay
Hymowitz.
        p.   cm.
Includes bibliographical references and index.
    ISBN 978-0-465-01842-0 (alk. paper)
    1. Men—United States—Psychology. 2. Emotional maturity—United
States. 3. Sex role—United States. 4. Feminism—United States. I. Title.
HQ1090.3.H96 2010
155.3'32—dc22   2010035842

10 9 8 7 6 5 4 3 2

To the memory of my mother,
Emily Sunstein

CONTENTS

INTRODUCTION
Adolescence Redux

Where have the good men gone? I'll bet you've heard some version of that question before. Laura Nolan, a common-sensical British woman in her thirties who lived in New York for five years and would like a husband and children but is hardly what you'd call desperate, put it this way: "We have an overload of man-boys—which leaves a generation of single, thirtysomething women who are their natural mates bewildered. . . . An odd thing happens to man-boy brains at about the age of 30. Some neural pathway, hitherto well oiled through a diet of normal relationships and an awareness of such terms as 'compromise' and 'I'm sorry,' tunes in to a specific area of the brain labeled 'navel-gazing.'"[1]

Next time she's in New York, Nolan might like to have coffee with Julie Klausner, comedian and author of *I Don't Care About Your Band*, and one of many similarly disgruntled American women, though their beef is more often with men in their twenties. "We are sick of hooking up with guys," she writes, and by "guys" she means males who are not boys or men but something else entirely. "Guys talk about *Star Wars* like it's not a movie made for people half their age; a guy's idea of a perfect night is to hang

1

around the PlayStation with his bandmates, or a trip to Vegas with his college friends. Guys feed you Chipotle and ride their bikes in traffic. They are more like the kids we babysat than the dads who drove us home." One female reviewer of Klausner's touchingly funny book wrote, "I had to stop several times while reading and think: wait, did I date this same guy?"[2]

Not so long ago, average mid-twentysomethings, both male and female, had achieved most of the milestones of adulthood: high school diploma, financial independence, marriage, and children. These days, they hang out in a novel sort of limbo, a hybrid state of semi-hormonal adolescence and responsible self-reliance. The limbo—I'll be calling it preadulthood—has much to recommend it, especially for the college-educated men I'll be writing about in this book. But it seems about time to state what has become obvious to legions of frustrated young women: it doesn't tend to bring out the best in men. I know what you're thinking: that description bears no resemblance to your prince of a son/nephew/friend/boyfriend. That may well be true. I've met a few such princes myself. Young men, like everything else in a postmodern world, come in many varieties, and there are numerous counterexamples to the child-man. But at this point, it's looking pretty clear that ten or fifteen years of party-on single life are a good formula for producing navel-gazing, wisecracking childmen rather than unhyphenated, unironic men.

To understand why that is, we need to take a good look at this cultural habitat of preadulthood. Decades in the unfolding, the limbo of the twenty- and early thirtysomething years probably strikes many readers as not especially noteworthy. After all, the media has been crowded with preadults for almost two decades. Adolescents saturated the cultural imagination from Elvis in the 1950s to the Beatles in the 1960s to John Hughes in the 1980s, but by the 1990s the media jilted the teen for the twentysomething. Movies started the affair in the early 1990s with such titles as *Singles*, *Reality Bites*, *Single White Female*, and *Swingers*. Television soon deepened the relationship. Monica, Joey, Rachel, and Ross; Jerry and Elaine; Carrie, Miranda, et al.: these singles were the most popular characters on television in the United States and just about everywhere else on the globe where people own televisions.

But despite its familiar media presence, preadulthood represents a momentous sociological development, much as the appearance of adolescence did in the early twentieth century. It's not exaggerating things to say that large numbers of single, young men and women living independently while also carrying enough disposable income in their wallets to avoid ever messing up their kitchens is something entirely new to human experience. The vast majority of humans have spent their lives as part of families—first, the one created by their own parents, and then soon after that, the one they entered through marriage—for the simple reason that no one (well, almost no one) could survive on their own. Yes, during other points in Western history, young people waited to marry until their mid- and sometimes even their later twenties (though almost never living independently before they wed), and yes, office girls and bachelor lawyers have been working and finding amusement in cities for more than a century. But their numbers and their money supply were small enough to keep them minor players in both the social ecology and the economy. Preadults are a different matter: they are a major demographic event.

What also makes preadulthood something new and big—and what begins to explain why the "Where have the good men gone?" question won't go away—is its radical reversal of the sexual hierarchy. Among preadults, women are the first sex. Women

3

graduate from college in greater numbers than men, with higher grade point averages; more extracurricular experiences, including study abroad; and as most professors tell it, more confidence, drive, and plans for the future. They are aggressively independent; they don't need to rely on any man, that's for sure. These strengths carry them through much of their twenties, when they are more likely to be in grad school and making strides in the workplace, to be buying apartments and otherwise in aspiring mode. In an increasing number of cities, they are even outearning their brothers and boyfriends.

By contrast, men can come across as aging frat boys, maladroit geeks, or unwashed slackers. The gender gap was crystallized—or perhaps caricatured is the better word—by the director Judd Apatow in his hit 2007 movie *Knocked Up* through his 23-year-old hero Ben Stone and Alison, the woman Ben accidentally impregnates after a drunken meeting at a club. Ben lives in a Los Angeles crash pad with a group of grubby friends who spend their days playing video games, smoking pot, and unsuccessfully planning the launch of their porn website. Alison, though hardly a matron, makes Ben look as if he's still in middle school. She is on her way up as a reporter at E! Entertainment network and lives in an apartment in the guesthouse of her sister's well-appointed home with what appear to be clean sheets and towels. Once she decides to have the baby, she figures out what needs to be done and does it. Either under the influence of mind-altering substances or in his natural state of goofball befuddlement, Ben can only stumble his way to responsible adulthood.

Here we have the two sexes of young urban singlehood, male and female, one lazy, crude, and immature, the other put-together, smart, and ambitious. (Think also of Bart and Lisa Simpson, Anthony and Meadow Soprano, and the male and female characters in just about every coed commercial on television.) Skeptics will be quick to object that these are just popular-culture confections, and so they are. But they reflect real trends in the predicament of the sexes in the contemporary world. Articles and books with such titles as "The End of Men," "Are Men Necessary?," *The Decline of Males,* "The Death of Macho," "Women Will Rule the World," and *Is There Anything Good About Men?* point toward a growing recognition that men are not thriving in today's cultural and economic environment. Preadulthood, a time of life when the middle-class kids first become independent, when after two decades of high-stakes schooling and helicopter parenting no one is telling them when papers are due or summer vacation starts, when, in short, the future is finally pretty much in their own hands, should be able to cast fresh light on the question of what's-the-matter-with-guys-today.

So where did preadults come from? Reading media reports, especially those about men, you might assume it's because spoiled 24-year-olds are trying to prolong the campus drinking and hook-up scene, while keeping the Bank of Mom and Dad in business. They might cite as evidence the 2010 healthcare bill, which extends until age 26 the eligibility of "dependent children" to stay on their parents' insurance plans. But preadulthood is not even remotely a college after-party. It's an adjustment to huge shifts in the economy, one that makes a college education essential to achieving or maintaining a middle-class life. Economists tell us that beginning in the 1980s, the economic advantage to higher education began to increase. Between 1960 and 2000, the percentage of 20-, 25-, and 30-year-old Americans enrolled in school more than doubled. Not only has college enrollment climbed to unprecedented rates but so have the numbers of students in graduate school. The reason is simple: in the "knowledge economy," good jobs go to those with degrees. And degrees take years.

More central to the lengthening of the road to adulthood is an increasingly labyrinthine labor market. In Chapter 1, we'll be looking at scores of job categories that did not exist ten or twenty years ago, or if they did, had so few members as to appear to be impossible professions. Both the economic expansion between the mid-1980s and 2007 and the digital revolution have transformed the high-end labor market into a highly competitive, high-stakes, sometimes scary mega-amusement park. Consider this one example: when baby boomers such as myself reached their twenties, there were three television networks—apart from a barely noticed PBS—all of them presided over by Walter Cronkite or his clones. Today there are hundreds of networks ranging from the high-minded C-SPAN to the ribald Comedy Central. We tend to look at this development from a consumer's perspective. Skeptics worry about the distractions of an ADD-contaminated remote control; enthusiasts praise a media promising so much individual choice. If you think about those 300 channels from the point of view of the young worker-to-be, however, you'll probably want to side with the enthusiasts. All of those networks need writers, set designers, advertisers, executive producers, senior producers, segment producers, coordinating field producers, web designers, directors, actors, editors, voice-over performers, and on-air talking heads. They might cut some of those jobs during bad economic times, as they are doing as I write, but the point remains: the past decades have seen a labor-market explosion of jobs to stir the ambitions of aspiring young grads.

Getting a solid foothold on the lower rung of these careers can take young wannabes many years. For one thing, many of these jobs are stimulating, creative, adventurous, or even glamorous, which means they are also highly competitive, more so than ever now that the economy has worsened. Career reality shows such as *Top Chef*, *Project Runway*, and *Top Design*, as well as that not-so-real reality show *Next Great Artist* (on those new cable channels that have expanded the entertainment job market, by the way), reflect the fascination with the dog-eat-dog struggle to make it in appealing creative careers. Jobs that attract young men and women on the make also often require years of moving between school and internships, between internships and jobs, laterally and horizontally between jobs, and between cities in the United States and abroad. Adding to the duration of the career search is the arcane nature of so many of these new positions. Even highly educated parents don't know, and probably in many cases counselors are in the dark about, the answers to such questions as: How does a young grad go about becoming a content strategist? (For that matter, what *is* a content strategist?) How about a design anthropologist? Or a script supervisor?

The Great Recession will doubtless temper youthful optimism on this score, but the knowledge economy gives the educated young an unprecedented opportunity to think about work in personal terms. They can seek out careers—not just jobs, mind you, which are a far less existential matter—to exercise their talents and "passions," an unlikely but commonplace word in the contemporary twentysomething career discussion. They expect these careers to give shape to their identity. In their thinking, "What do you do?" is almost synonymous with "Who are you?" It is the self in action, or so the theory goes.

Preadulthood, then, is the new adolescence not just because it has taken over the prime-time sitcom schedule but also because it is the contemporary stage for young men and women to deal with the big questions about their lives. The similarities are worth considering for a moment. Starting in the mid-twentieth century, adolescence extended childhood until 18 as American teenagers were herded away from the fields and the workplace and into that new institution, the high school. For a long time, the poor and recent immigrants were not part of adolescent life; they went straight to work because their families couldn't afford the lost labor and income. But overall, the country had grown rich enough to carve out space and time to create a more highly educated citizenry and workforce.[3] Teenagers quickly became a marketing and cultural phenomenon. They also earned their own psychological profile. One of the most influential of the psychologists of adolescence was Erik Erikson, who described the stage as a "moratorium," a limbo between childhood and adulthood characterized by role confusion, emotional turmoil, and identity conflict.

As with adolescents in the twentieth century, preadults have been waitlisted for adulthood. Preadulthood is also a response to particular social and economic conditions that create much uncertainty and angst.[4] A demanding economy lengthened adolescence, already an extension of childhood, into the decade or more of preadulthood. Marketers and culture-creators help promote preadulthood as a lifestyle (including, but hardly limited to, sex, drugs, and rock and roll.) Similar to adolescence, preadulthood is a class-based social phenomenon reserved for the relatively well-to-do. Poor and working-class twentysomethings who don't get a four-year college degree are not in a position to compete for the more satisfying jobs of the knowledge economy. Their trajectory during the years before adulthood is its own more troubling story, one that will have to be a subject for a different book.[5]

Preadults differ in one major respect from adolescents. They write their own biographies—and from scratch. Sociologists have a useful term: "life script."[6] It refers to a particular society's ordering of large life events. Though life scripts vary according to a society's economy and culture, the archetypal plot is deeply rooted in our biological nature. It starts with infancy and childhood. Puberty, or sexual maturity, then signals readiness for marriage and child-rearing, as well as for what were almost always gender-based work requirements. Inexorably, next came waning fertility, declining health, and demise. As societies grew more complex, the period between sexual maturity and marriage elongated, as it did when adolescence became a common part of the life story. But adolescence did not change the large Roman numerals of the script. Adults continued to be those who took over the primary tasks of the economy and culture. For women, the central task usually involved the day-to-day rearing of the next generation; for men, the protection of and provision for their wives and children. Follow the script and become an adult, a temporary custodian, until your own old age and death, of the social order.

Unlike adolescents, however, preadults don't know what is supposed to come next. They're not sure what the gender scripts are, if there are any. They're not even sure what the word "adult" means.[7] We've already seen how tangled the route to adult work identity has become. Marriage and parenthood also come in many forms or can be skipped altogether. No wonder, then, that a lot of twenty- or thirtysomethings find themselves suffering through a "quarterlife crisis," a period of depression and worry over the shape of their lives. With no life outline to rely on, they struggle with their own private development hell.

Given the import and rigors of contemporary career-building along with the copious choices that have to be pondered, preadults who do marry and start families do so later than ever before in human history, just as they often—though far less than media reports suggest—move back in with their parents. Husbands or wives and children (and apartments) are a drag on the footloose life required along the early career track and identity search. Preadulthood has also confounded the primordial search for a mate. It has delayed a stable sense of identity, dramatically expanded the pool of possible spouses, mystified courtship routines, and helped to throw into doubt the very meaning of marriage.

For women especially, late marriage represents a paradigm shift, a revolution in both behavior and values. Up until very recently, the central fact about a woman in her twenties and early thirties was that she was a wife and mother, whether a 23-year-old from Ming, China, or a 26-year-old in Mad Men, America. Most human beings have had to endure a standard of living where a woman, or man for that matter, would have trouble surviving on her or his own; this is still the case today in the undeveloped world, where girls are married off by the age of 18 or considerably younger by parents eager to have one fewer mouth to feed. History is varied enough that there were some women who did not marry and lived with relatives, who didn't marry until their mid-twenties (the norm in northeast Europe through much of the early modern period), who couldn't conceive, or who had other important social roles as well as motherhood. They were the exceptions. Even in the United States in 1970, college graduates were married within a year of graduation, that is, before they turned 23, and the large majority went on to have children after a year or two.[8]

Today's college-educated 23-year-old woman, of course, has other plans. Big plans. In a complete reversal of the expectations of their female ancestors and even their own mothers, marriage and children for preadult women are optional, or at any rate not anything to be thinking about now. What is not optional is the same for both women and men: finding work that will bring meaning and money to their lives. By large margins, young women say it is very important that they be "economically set" before they even consider getting married.[9] Women's determination to achieve financial independence before marriage is something very new, and it is at the very heart of preadulthood.

People generally chalk up the revolution in women's ambitions to three interrelated forces: the birth control pill, feminism, and changes in discrimination law. As we'll see in Chapter 2, the explanation is true but incomplete. To make work central to their lives, young women may have had to escape sexism and unplanned pregnancies, but they also had to be freed from the demands of ordinary preindustrial life. Thanks to what is sometimes called the second industrial revolution, that freedom was on its way considerably before the pill hit pharmacy shelves. In the mid-nineteenth century, improved contraceptives were reducing the number of children keeping women confined. By the early twentieth century, women, and men for that matter, were being relieved of other ancient forms of domestic labor by textile mills, household electricity, indoor plumbing, factory-made food goods, and the like. At the same time, medical advances helped women escape the debilitating injuries that so frequently followed childbirth. Second-wave feminism transformed the American scene beginning in the mid-1960s only after middle-class women had thoroughly overcome the miseries of preelectrical, pre–indoor plumbing, and pre-antibiotic domestic life. And only then could they responsibly raise daughters who would put work at the center of their ambitions.

And that's exactly what they did. Feminist-influenced mothers and fathers began grooming their daughters for the workplace like prize horses. To some extent, their zeal was related to the larger phenomenon commonly called "soccer" parenting, which has kept both girls *and* boys busier than CEOs. Preparing their kids for the competition for name-brand college degrees that would lead to the best knowledge economy jobs, parents treated their kids like top athletes training for the gold. They hovered over their homework and hauled them from swim practice to violin lessons to drama club.[10] By the 1990s, as experts warned of a crisis in female self-esteem, girls became the particular focus of parents' obsessions. Cultural institutions and marketers joined to celebrate girl power; even the government became a "you-go-girl" cheering section. Girls could be anything they wanted: astronaut, biochemist, president, or speaker of the House. Unlike the damsels of the past, they should not bother their brainy heads with thoughts of marriage and children. With some effort, they could become what psychologist Dan Kindlon calls "alpha girls."[11] And for alphas, independence and career success were—and are—the goal.

For the scenario to work, there had to be not just an end to self-doubt but also a large inventory of gratifying, high-paying jobs. It made no sense to spend so much energy grooming girls to struggle for secretarial jobs or for a very limited number of law and editorial positions. Chapter 3's subject is the continuing technological and economic progress that produced the sorts of jobs to make women happily career-minded. Globalization, improved productivity, and a digital revolution propelled a massive shift in the economy, away from manufacturing to knowledge and services—to women's great advantage. "The post-industrial economy is indifferent to men's size and strength," explains Hanna Rosin in her popular article "The End of Men."[12] The knowledge economy, by contrast, multiplies opportunities in such fields as law, media, public relations, fashion, graphic and product design, book publishing, communications, and retail, where the few women who had pursued careers in the past had generally gravitated.

Academics have seriously understated just how much this economic and technological shift has provided the infrastructure for feminist success. These shifts helped to proliferate new media while also flooding the market with cheap consumer goods. We've already seen an example of how contemporary media, with all of its current options, has expanded the labor market for educated young workers. The arrival of so many cheap consumer goods had the same effect. Shoes, sofas, refrigerators, MP3 players, and all of the other goodies now affordable for just about everyone in developed economies need to be designed, advertised, branded, contracted, and capitalized. The companies producing them have to have managers, planners, public relations specialists, lawyers, and accountants.

Some analysts have suggested that men are less suited than women to some of these jobs, particularly those in communication and design. These are jobs that rely on such avowedly "female" traits as aesthetic awareness, sensitivity, intuition, and a willingness to collaborate—not to mention a consumer mindset. (As busy as they are writing copy or diagnosing a lung disease, women remain the dominant consumers.) Whether these qualities are innately feminine or not, this much is clear: in most knowledge jobs, including leadership positions whose requirements now emphasize "emotional intelligence," women are easily men's equals. It's worth noting that the success of young women has become an international affair, creating what I'll be calling the New Girl Order. Women are outperforming men in school and entry-level jobs even in such places as South Korea, Poland, and China. Why? These countries never had a vocal feminist movement—but they do have a growing knowledge sector.

That brings us at last to the question of where the good men have gone. The preadult guy story is rather different from that for women. Yes, men have found plenty of cool jobs in the knowledge economy. They continue to pursue careers in journalism, law, medicine, publishing, and government, of course, though they are now the minority in some of those fields. It's striking, however, how much the workplace has been segregated. Far more than anyone might have predicted, in the twenty-first century knowledge economy and even among the college educated, a lot of guys continue to do "guy stuff" and a lot of girls, "girl stuff." Young men dominate the hugely expanded tech sector; the immense video game industry is also the happy home for many young men. They are the majority force in the testosterone-infected financial domain and at the dozen or so sports channels.

Still, by most accounts, young men are not showing the same focus or resilience that supervisors and professors notice among women. This is not the case for all men by any means. Plenty of guys graduate college with a résumé to rival or surpass the most enterprising alpha girls. But there is a large and prominent group of men who hit their twenties and seem unsure what's expected of them.

Chapters 4 and 5 delve into the mystery of what I call the child-man, the cultural antithesis of the alpha girl. Preadulthood was a product of trends that took shape in the middle of the twentieth century but peaked in the 1990s. The child-man took a similarly long time to materialize. Men have been struggling with finding an acceptable adult male identity since at least the mid-nineteenth century. We often hear about the miseries of women confined to the domestic sphere once men began to work in offices and factories away from home. It seems that men didn't much like the arrangement either. They balked at the stuffy propriety of the bourgeois parlor as they did later at the banal activities of the suburban living room. They turned to hobbies and adventures, such as hunting and fishing. In the midcentury, fathers who had refused to put down the money to buy those newfangled televisions when they first arrived in stores changed their minds when the networks began broadcasting boxing matches and baseball games. The arrival in the 1950s of *Playboy* seemed like the ultimate protest against male domestication—think of the refusal of adult manhood implied by the title alone.

The playboy was a prologue for the contemporary child-man in his disregard for domestic life. Unlike the playboy with his jazz- and art-filled pads, however, the boy rebel of today is a creature of the animal house. In the 1990s, *Maxim*, the hugely popular rude and lewd "lad" magazine, arrived from England. Its philosophy and tone were so juvenile, so entirely undomesticated, it made *Playboy* look like Camus. By the 2000s, young men were tuning in to such cable channels as Comedy Central, the Cartoon Network, and Spike, whose shows reflected the adolescent male preferences of its targeted male audiences. They watched movies with such overgrown boy actors as Steve Carrell, Luke and Owen Wilson, Jim Carrey, Adam Sandler, Will Ferrell, and Seth Rogen, the star of the aforementioned *Knocked Up*, and cheered their awesome car crashes, fart jokes, breast and crotch shots, explosions, beer pong competitions, and other frat-boy pranks. Americans had always struck foreigners as youthful, even childlike, in their energy and optimism. But this? This was something different—not just youthful but, quite literally, retarded.

Commentators most commonly describe these juvenile predilections as evidence of a media-inspired backlash against feminism. Boys went to school thinking they were going on a journey to the top jobs, goes the theory, and what they got instead was a girl-powered campus and labor market. They have rebelled by pledging themselves to the Guy Code—the term comes from the sociologist Michael Kimmel—treating women as objects of hormonal revenge and making "you're-so-gay" quips with their bros.[13] But child-men, as we've seen, have a long Western pedigree. They don't look much like a disappointed ruling class, especially the awkward geeks and sad-sack emo-boys in their ranks. If you watch closely, you'll notice a meta-quality to the child-man media, whether *Maxim* or Will Ferrell's *Old School*, a tendency to wink at the contemporary man's shallowness and puerility, as if the dudes know full well just how ridiculous they are.

More likely, the child-man is a reaction to a widespread cultural uncertainty about men, an uncertainty considerably aggravated by preadulthood. It's been an almost universal rule of civilization that whereas girls became women simply by reaching physical maturity, boys had to pass a test. They needed to demonstrate courage, physical prowess, or mastery of the necessary skills. The goal was to prove their competence as protectors of women and children; this was always their primary social role. Today, however, with women moving ahead in an advanced economy, provider husbands and fathers are now optional, and the character qualities men had needed to play their role—fortitude, stoicism, courage, fidelity— are obsolete and even a little embarrassing.

This makes the preadult man something like an actor in a drama in which he only knows what he shouldn't say. He has to compete in a fierce job market but can't act too bossy or self-confident. He should be sensitive but not paternalistic, smart but not cocky. To deepen his predicament, because he is single, his advisers and confidants are generally undomesticated dudes just like him. Single men have never been civilization's most responsible actors; they continue to be more troubled and less successful than men who deliberately choose to become husbands and fathers. If, without an adult male playbook, some of them live in rooms decorated with *Star Wars* posters and crushed beer cans and treat women like disposable estrogen toys, well, we can be disgusted, but we shouldn't be surprised.

This is the not-very-promising background for preadult men and women as they look for sex and love, the subject of Chapter 6. Whether in private conversations with their friends or on web-sites with such names as Relationshit.com, Heartlessbitches.com, and Dating-is-hell.net, they list their complaints. Women say guys are immature, uncivil, and utterly unfathomable. Men appear interested in them, even eager; they make plans for future dates to go to concerts and dinner or even a ski trip to Colorado together, and then suddenly and inexplicably stop answering messages. (One young woman I know was so puzzled by one of these disappearing acts that she checked the obituaries.) Men grouse about women who can't decide if they want equality or chivalry. One day a woman gives you the evil eye for opening the door for her; the next, she is annoyed if you text instead of call.

Once men and women are equals, many of the old rules of dating don't make sense any more. Those rules are hanging around anyway. Though they may make less money than women, men are still expected to pick up the restaurant or bar check, at least in the early stages of a relationship. Women may sleep with you on a first date if they don't care if they see you again, but may "save themselves" if they do. Women want chocolates on Valentine's Day— or better yet, a weekend in Paris. After a few years of dating in their first years out of college, a lot of men begin to suspect that women are not as new a breed as had been advertised. Yes, they can be as casual about sex as the guys in the locker room. No, they're not just husband-hunting, especially in their twenties. Still, they seem strangely indifferent to the sensitive, nice guys that parents and teachers assured boys was the way to a liberated woman's heart. The putative disconnect between what women say they want and the men they actually choose has led to a thriving industry of gurus and dating coaches teaching child-men to become "pick-up artists." According to their theory, which is commonly described as "game," women prefer domineering, alpha men. To find women, men have to project confidence, vigor, and a hint of aloof mystery, precisely the qualities they had been warned against by their mothers and teachers.

Whether devotees of game are right or not, one thing is clear: ancient habits continue to break through postcollegiate gender ideals like weeds through cracks in the pavement. Educated women may fool around with their trainers, but even the highest-paid attorneys and businesswomen will tie the knot only with men who are (at least) their status equals. It is true that college-educated men are no longer marrying their pretty secretaries or nurses. They want highly educated wives who will help them produce children with the smarts needed for the competitive knowledge economy. Though preadults say they will only settle for soul mates, they barter their way through the mating market in ways that would bring a knowing smile to Edith Wharton's face. Here's just one charming example: the Ivy Plus Society, a networking group that "brings together young alumni from a select group of schools to create a community of talented, dynamic individuals." Translation: no one here wants to date losers from state universities or such second-tier colleges as Sarah Lawrence and Bowdoin. "I've been in the city three years and dated girls who are legitimate models, and that gets old," one member who works in private equity told the *New York Times* in an article about the society. "I have high standards."[14]

The gap between preadult ideals and Darwinian realities only widens as women reach their thirties. Thirtysomething women, such as Laura Nolan and Julie Klausner whom we met at the beginning of this introduction, face a painful contradiction: by 35, their fertility is in decline. As some cruel god would have it, that's the same time they confront a diminishing pool of interested men. Social attitudes toward working women may have undergone a revolution, but the rules of sex appeal have not. As women move into their thirties and forties, they remain less enticing to younger men than men of that age are to younger women. Men who at 23 may have felt like the class dork find their stride by 30. Women are on the opposite trajectory. Sexism? Evolution? It doesn't really matter; it's not going away.

Between his lack of familial responsibilities, his relative affluence, and an entertainment media devoted to his every pleasure, the single young man can live in pig's heaven—and he often does. He has plenty of time—at least he thinks so from his sad little apartment—to become a mensch. Women put up with him for a while, but then in fear and disgust they either decide to change their plans and give up on the husband and kids or they go to the sperm bank and get the DNA without the troublesome child-man attached. They're probably not thinking about it this way, but their choice only legitimizes the guy's attachment to the sandbox. Why should he grow up? No one needs him anyway. He has nothing he's got to do.

Might as well grab the remote and have another beer.

one

PREADULTS AND THEIR BRILLIANT CAREERS

What should I do with my life? Good question. As it happens, it's also the title of a popular 2002 book by writer Po Bronson. *What Should I Do With My Life?* spent twenty-two weeks on the best-seller list as a hardcover; as a paperback it hung around for another twelve. More than seven years later, it's *still* going strong.[1]

There's a good reason for that. Bronson's book taps into a remarkable but poorly understood shift in American life. Today in the United States and in much of the developed world, people—especially educated, middle-class people—can ask that question and answer it however they want. This may seem like a banal observation, a little like noting that Burger King customers can "have it their way." It's not. As a mass phenomenon, a largely open-ended what-should-I-do-with-my-life question is a cultural novelty, one that has fundamentally transformed the life script for a good chunk of the American population.

For, as many twenty- and thirtysomethings and their dismayed parents are discovering, searching for an answer to the question means taking a lot longer to grow up. In the past, the young followed a script that everyone tacitly understood and only a few outliers veered from. In preindustrial and even to a large extent in industrial societies, no one asked "What do you want to do with your life?" because with minor exceptions, no one was in a position to ask. People knew within certain parameters what work they would do, where they would live, in which tribe or religion or village or town they would find their wives or husbands, and how they would raise their kids, who would likely follow the same path as they did when they grew up. In many parts of the world— think of most of Africa, the Middle East, rural Asia, and some religious communities in the United States—life continues to unfold in this way.

In the United States since the middle of the twentieth century, the usual biography went like this: 1. childhood and schooling; 2. adolescence and end of schooling; 3. a job (for men always, for women sometimes); 4. marriage; 5. children; and 6. old age and the great beyond. There were individual choices within the confines of the script. Number 4, for instance, the identity of one's spouse, was a major decision in people's lives. People generally made that decision in their early or mid-twenties, meaning by that time—certainly by thirty—they were full-fledged grown-ups, settled and already raising the next generation to follow the same script they had.

By contrast, today in your twenties and early thirties you are probably still only booting up. These are the years you figure out what to do with your life, to write the outlines of your own personal biography, and in the current environment, that takes some trial and error. Young people wander from job to job while they try to decide what kind of career they want. They move from apartment to apartment, city to city, country to country, sometimes adding an extensive pit stop in their childhood bedrooms, while they figure out where they want to settle. They go through one-night stands, dates, girlfriends and boyfriends, multiyear live-in relationships, breakups, and even "starter marriage" divorces while they decide with whom, if anyone, they should spend their lives. They decide when to start a family. Or they decide never to start a family. You write your own script, design your own plan. "Work How You Want, Live Where You Want, Be What You Want to Be," goes the motto of a website weirdly but not inaccurately called "the Untemplater."

The slow road to adulthood has been under construction since the late 1960s but only in the last ten years have its main features become clear enough for social scientists to conclude that we are witnessing the appearance of a new stage of life. The twentieth century gave us adolescence; the twenty-first—give or take a decade—is giving us the single twenty- and thirtysomething. Jeffrey Arnett, a professor at the University of Maryland whose books and conferences make him the top academic entrepreneur on the topic, has labeled the phase "emerging adulthood." Others refer to "the transition to adulthood," or "not quite adults."[2] The popular media has tried out terms like "adultescence," "quarterlife," "boomerang generation," and "twixters."[3]

I prefer the term *preadulthood*. Without stable employment, quasi-permanent independent residence, wives, husbands, or children, "adult" seems premature. Preadults themselves have the feeling of being in transition. True, these days 50- or 60-year-olds might grapple with the same sentiment, but they're kidding themselves. Even today when grown-ups commonly divorce and remarry, retrain, and move from Boston to Seattle, we still think of the adult as having a stable identity. Preadults, on the other hand, are undefined and unformed. Neuroscientists would confirm the truth of this for at least younger twentysomethings because their brains are still developing.[4] They may be legally adults and, if necessary, capable of fending entirely for themselves, but they lack the social identity that comes with being settled into a home, occupation, and marital family that humans have almost always associated with adult maturity. Preadults are not there yet.

Scholars were not the only ones to sense the arrival of an important new demographic. Savvy marketers and Hollywood creatives also smelled preadult spirit. By the mid-1990s, instead of invading the 'burbs after marrying and having baby number one, armies of single twenty- and thirtysomethings went the other direction, into American cities, to ponder what to do with their lives. Much to the advantage of other city-dwellers, they transformed such neighborhoods as Murray Hill and Williamsburg in New York; much of Austin, Texas; Capitol Hill in Seattle; Logan Square in Chicago; and just about anywhere in Portland, a city that by the early 2000s was the mecca of preadult professionals.[5] Because of the happy demographic collision of preadulthood and increased immigration during that decade, modestly priced Thai, Indian, and Mexican restaurants sprouted up throughout these areas; it helped that preadults adore spicy food, a reflection of their youthful desire for adventure and their multicultural childhoods. They also lured new cocktail bars, Starbucks, gyms, shoe boutiques, and gift stores where they could buy scented candles for their apartments and tote bags for their trips to Costa Rica and Istanbul. Preadults may be saddled with college debt, but they have considerably more disposable cash than people of other ages at the same income level.[6]

Advertisers understood this well because during the same decade of the 1990s, television shows about young, single adults rolled out one after another: *Melrose Place, Ally McBeal, ER, The Real World, Friends, Seinfeld,* and eventually *Sex and the City.* Preadults weren't just exploring the question of what to do with their lives; they hadn't just moved to former working-class, urban neighborhoods with cheap ethnic food eateries. They were inventing a new lifestyle for the entire country—actually, the entire world, given the global popularity of these shows—to admire.

So why do we have a new stage of life, why Williamsburg and Portland at this time and in this country? There's one reason above all, one that no one has fully fleshed out: preadulthood, the time for exploring the question "What should I do with my life?" is a predictable, perhaps even necessary, response to massive changes in the way Americans earn a living. The preadult is a child, in multiple senses of the word, of what is known as the knowledge economy.

It's a wonky term, *knowledge economy*, but there's no way to grasp the predicament of those young urbanites without wrestling with it. By the late 1960s and for the decades that followed, the Western world produced a growing number of jobs trading in knowledge and ideas rather than brawn, manual dexterity, or routine clerical skills. These were knowledge jobs mostly in the fields of technology, medicine, law, design, culture, and finance. In 1959, Peter Drucker, the brilliant management theorist, or "social ecologist" as he liked to call himself, foresaw the coming of the new economy in his book *Landmarks of Tomorrow*.[7] Decades later, his prescience was clear; by the mid-1990s, knowledge workers made up a third of the American workforce. Despite America's romance with the lunchbox worker and the periodic call to "buy American," their numbers were greater than the country's industrial laborers at any point in its history outside of wartime.[8]

Let's look at some examples of the kinds of jobs we're talking about. Between 1960 and 2000, the number of lawyers per capita doubled from approximately 1 in 627 to 1 in 300. Over the same period, the percentage of the total workforce made up of managers, officials, and proprietors climbed from 8 to 14 percent; the percentage made up of professional and technical workers doubled from 12 to nearly 25.[9] MBA degrees soared by 310 percent between 1974 and 2000.[10] Overall, between 1970 and 2003, creative work, in policy analyst Richard Florida's perhaps overly flattering words, increased by 50 percent as a percentage of the U.S. economy.[11] When looking at knowledge workers, we may be talking about a privileged class, but it is now a very large privileged class.

Observers correctly point to one central reason that the knowledge economy means a longer, more chaotic trip to adulthood. As its name suggests, a knowledge economy relies on people with a lot of knowledge, or more precisely, a lot of education, which may or may not be the same thing.[12] In the big-factory era, many Americans understandably viewed college as a luxury item, a finishing school for well-to-do wives-to-be and a holding pen for otherwise-idle rich boys.[13] In 1960, barely 8 percent of the population had a bachelor's degree. For that matter, nearly 60 percent of American adults lacked a high school diploma.[14] That made sense, given that two-fifths of the American workforce was made up of, in Drucker's words, "industrial workers who make or move things."[15] But by the late 1960s, with a growing number of jobs requiring thinking and analyzing, parents began to view studying for a BA or BS as a practical decision, even if it did mean paying tuition and housing for four extra years. Over the next decades, education levels skyrocketed. By 2000, the percentage of the population with a four-year college degree had almost tripled to 24 percent. Today, the percentage of college grads is near 30 percent and is growing.[16]

More dramatic still was the increase in the number of people getting graduate degrees. Sociologists Barbara Schneider and David

Stevenson found a stunning rise throughout the 1980s in the number of high school seniors who aspired to a professional occupation. These aspirations were not just teenage castles in the sky; between 1985 and 2007, graduate school enrollment jumped a remarkable 67 percent.[17] Typically, middle-class students graduate from college at 21 or 22, which should give them plenty of time to settle down by 24 or so even if that includes a year of bumming around the ski slopes or traveling to Africa. Postgraduate training is another matter. It can go on well into the twenties or, in the case of, say, surgeons or PhDs, into the thirties. One result? Preadulthood.

The growth in both college and graduate degrees came almost entirely from the female half of the population, a fact whose consequences we will be pondering in the following chapters. After 1970, the fraction of men with four-year college degrees in the United States stalled; the percentage of women with these degrees, meanwhile, exploded. In 1970, women earned 40 percent of college degrees. By 1980, they had reached a par with men, and by 2006, they had catapulted ahead, earning 57 percent of the four-year degrees in the United States.[18]

At this point, there are two reigning theories about the causes of this particular gender gap. The first has it that boys develop more slowly, especially when it comes to verbal skills. Starting out behind, boys never catch up to their literate and talkative sisters.[19] The other theory puts it in less academic terms. Girls have superior "noncognitive abilities"; they're more organized, pay more attention in class, do their homework, and don't horse around. Interestingly enough, whichever theory you believe—or if you believe a little of both, which seems a reasonable proposition—the phenomenon has become global. Women earn more college degrees than men in 67 of 120 nations, including 17 poor countries—and even in fundamentalist Iran.[20]

For both women and men, the main reason for college fervor isn't hard to guess. The jobs available to degreed students are better jobs. They command higher salaries, more benefits, more generous pensions—and higher status. Economists use the term "college premium" to describe the economic advantages gained by those workers with a college diploma over those without. That premium grew dramatically after 1980. Today the median earning for a high school graduate is $33,000; compare that to the $56,000 earned by a college grad, and the $75,000 by those with an advanced degree.[21] Wages for men with less than a four-year college degree fell steeply over the past thirty years; during the same period, college-educated men earned 10 percent more. Not bad, but consider this: male workers with more than a bachelor's degree saw a 26 percent jump in earnings.[22] In addition to more money, college graduates get more respect—and security. Even though in a fast-paced global economy, no one is really job-certain, it remains true that employers tend to hang onto well-trained employees. It's much easier to find another bank teller than another tax lawyer. Teller skills are just not that hard or expensive to come by—either in terms of tuition dollars or time.

Understandably, the Great Recession has led more people to question the value of a college degree. Some economists believe jobs for white-collar workers are likely to become more unstable in character and fewer in number.[23] College pessimists also point out that the percentage of college grads with debt is at an all-time high, up from 49 in 1993 to 65 in 2007.[24] A flurry of books with such titles as *Generation Debt: Why Now Is a Terrible Time to Be Young* and *Strapped: Why America's Twenty and Thirtysomethings Can't Get Ahead* have argued that debt is a big part of the preadult story; people who owe tens of thousands of dollars, they observe, are in no position to start families or buy homes and may even feel the need to move in with their parents.

They've got a point. But it's easy to overstate how much debt explains the phenomenon of preadulthood. A recent College Board study, "Who Borrows Most?," found that only 17 percent of college grads have debt of $30,500 or more. Most of them come from middle-income, not poor, families who are more likely to be in a position to help their kids finesse the tight early years after college. The more typical college debtor owes $20,000 on graduation. Considering that our college grad is likely to earn considerably more than his less-educated peers, that should be a worthwhile burden. One prominent study found that most grads had paid off all but $7,000 three years out of college. As of 2000, most students were spending about 6 percent of their salary paying off debt, hardly a number to alter the life script.[25]

Granted, young college graduates have fared considerably worse than older educated workers during the downturn. In 2007, 84.4 percent of grads aged 22 to 27 had jobs, only somewhat lower than the 86.8 percent figure for college graduates aged 28 to 50. Since then, the employment gap between the two age groups has almost doubled. The intensified competition and continual adjustments that come with globalization are more apt to affect younger workers without seniority and established professional identity.

Still, though not immune to the havoc of the recession, the young worker with a college education is considerably better off than his non–college grad neighbor.[26] As of spring 2010, according to Richard Florida, the unemployment rate for college graduates remained less than 5 percent, well below the national average of more than 10 percent. The unemployment rate in the professional and technical fields—science and engineering, business and management, education and health care—was under 4 percent.[27] Barring a catastrophe, the future will continue to belong to knowledge workers. The management consultancy firm McKinsey & Company found that nearly 85 percent of new jobs created between 1998 and 2006 involved complex knowledge work.[28] That trend is not going to reverse itself. Over the next seven years, the U.S. Department of Labor expects the number of jobs in the information-technology sector to swell 24 percent—a figure more than twice the overall job-growth rate.[29] Job opportunities in mathematics and across the sciences are also expected to expand.[30] The U.S. Department of Labor projects that network systems, data communications, and computer software engineering will be the highest-growth occupations by 2016.

More money, more benefits, more hope, more stability, more prestige: these are good reasons to spend years in a library or lab and put off a steady paycheck until age 22 or, if grad school is in the cards, 27-plus. But there's another explanation for why the knowledge economy has led to preadulthood. The new economy, especially since the computer and Internet revolution of the 1990s, produces jobs of amazing complexity and variety. It takes a really long time to figure out how it all works and where you fit in.

This wasn't so true in the early days of the knowledge economy thirty or forty years ago. In 1970, when I was graduating from a private liberal arts college, my friends considered about five different sorts of careers that would be both interesting to them and consistent with their lifestyle—or status—expectations. Just about all of them became doctors, lawyers, professors, psychologists, or journalists. In very rare and enviable cases, they found careers as filmmakers or photographers. This was the decade that women began pouring into law and medical schools—not surprising, given these professions provided the most predictable and reliable path into the Before-Computer knowledge economy. Lisa Chamberlain, the Gen X author of *Slackonomics,* found a similar attitude for the generation that followed the boomers: "Growing up in the 1980s, it seemed anyone who didn't aspire to business school, law school, or medicine was destined for mediocrity."[31]

For Gen Y, or the millennials, as the generation now coming of age is commonly known, the situation has changed dramatically. The Before-Computer knowledge economy was a small boutique compared to the sprawling Mall of America millennials browse these days. We often read about jobs that have disappeared because of globalization and technological change. This is true for lower-skilled workers in particular. But the more striking story for the educated class over the past three decades—and especially in the past ten years—has been the opposite: a mega-kiloton explosion of career possibilities.

Here are some of the jobs that a millennial college grad can consider that did not exist when his parents were his age: web designer; video game developer; app creator; diversity administrator; video producer; systems analyst; software engineer; data communications analyst; biotech researcher; geneticist; microbiologist; contract specialist; content strategist; hedge fund investigator; human capital manager; environmental consultant; compensation consultant; info-graphic designer; design anthropologist; stager; strategic designer; user experience designer (UX); digital strategist; communications strategist; and any of the tens of thousands of administrative, technical, and strategic jobs at Google, Yahoo!, Sirius Radio, Microsoft, Apple, Starbucks, Amazon, Anthropologie, HBO, Comedy Central, MSNBC, MTV, or any of the hundreds of cable networks now entertaining us every day.

There are whole sectors of the economy that burst their seams in the past decades and poured out appealing job possibilities. Consider government jobs. The federal government is the nation's largest employer even without factoring in postal workers and passport clerks; about half of its workforce has a college degree.[32] A third of the federal government's 1.8 million employees are management, business, and financial workers, including accountants, auditors, and analysts. Another third are professionals—scientists, engineers (biological, environmental, nuclear, electrical, industrial, and aeronautical), lawyers, judges, law clerks, computer specialists, and administrators.[33] That's just on the federal level. State and local governments employ lawyers and finance specialists by the tens of thousands. Thirty years ago, you couldn't become the deputy secretary of one of the fifty state or municipal Departments of Environment because no such office existed. Today, in addition to administrators, there are thousands of environmental scientists and consultants working for state government.

Expanding government hasn't only meant more knowledge jobs in the public sphere. "Yahoo! Answers" asked visitors to "name at least 5 jobs that did not exist 10 years ago." The first commenter answered with one few people would think of: "Sarbanes-Oxley Compliance Manager," that is, an individual who makes sure a company's accounting procedures conform to the regulations of the 2002 Sarbanes-Oxley Act. Yes, and also compliance officers at private companies—many of them requiring a college education—for the thousands of local, state, and federal laws and regulations that have come on the books during the past forty years. Don't forget about the nonprofit sector. "Nonprofit work" is a common ambition on elite college campuses these days; it's also a category that barely anyone had conceptualized before 1990. No wonder. By the late 1990s, there were more than a million organizations registered in the United States as nonprofit or charitable groups doing social-sector work. The overwhelming majority of these—some 70 percent—had come into existence in the previous thirty years. Nonprofits grew more than 30 percent between 1998 and 2008, and as of 2006, they encompassed more than 8 percent of wages paid in the United States.[34]

Then there are interesting jobs that were around thirty years ago but were so few in number they barely registered on anyone's life-planning radar. Think about it: political risk consultant (someone who advises companies seeking to invest in foreign countries), graphic artist, shoe designer, yoga center director, forensic accountant (the person who digs into dubious company records to figure out if any executives better lawyer up; Franklin University, among others, offers a major in the subject), event planner, food stylist, organic food farmer, educational consultant, women's studies professor, venture capitalist, entertainment columnist, TV chef, political consultant, and pollster. Remember all those people going to college and graduate school who didn't in previous generations? In 1969, the total enrollment in degree-granting institutions in the United States was under a million. Today it is more than two and a quarter million.[35] Well, that means a lot of new teachers, deans, and diversity administrators. In the past ten years alone, law school faculties have increased by 40 percent with similar increases in the number of deans, librarians, and other full-time administrators.[36] There are scores upon scores of middle-management positions that people had barely heard of before 1980—human resources manager, brand manager, marketing manager, public relations manager, communications director. This is not to mention the lawyers and financial advisers for all of these new professionals.

Jobs in design have expanded so much that many people now refer to the "design economy." Think of the artsy kid of a generation

ago. The class doodler or tinkerer was an outcast who ranked somewhere above the tuba player and below the substitute goalie on the
hockey team in the school hierarchy. The design economy has
turned outsiders into cool kids with big futures. They can be
graphic, industrial, set, or web designers; or costume, dress, shoe,
handbag, children's clothes, furniture, wallpaper, tile, or toy designers. They can be strategic, font, user interface, video game, or info-
graphic designers. They can be creative or art directors, fashion or
food stylists, production or lighting artists, or animators. In the
1960s, we would have said these artists were selling out, but that
was before the design economy shattered the boundaries between
both art and business and the bohemian and the corporate.

Care for some more? As economic growth before the current downturn put more money in people's pockets, consumers
spent more on entertainment and leisure; consumer entertainment spending in 2009 accounted for 6 percent of household income as opposed to 3 percent in 1967.[37] More international travel
means more hotel and airline execs, cruise line managers, and
boat designers (the Cruise Line Association estimates that 118
of the 200 boats belonging to their members were built since
2000).[38] Here's another amazing statistic: the number of museums
went from 6,000 in 1976 to somewhere around (depending on
the definition of museum) 18,000 in 2006.[39] The Bureau of Labor
Statistics forecasts a 20 percent increase in the number of jobs
for curators, archivists, and museum technicians over the next
eight years.[40] Meanwhile, globalization and the Internet have increased the demand for film and video products. That means
more jobs for video artists, actors, comedians, directors, producers,
documentary filmmakers, and video game creators. During the
past decades, the number of regional theaters has soared from 23
in 1960 to 1,982 in 2005; it actually doubled between 1990 and

2005. Though some of those theaters are undoubtedly facing hard times—and maybe even closure—that still adds up to a lot more opportunities for aspiring theater folks.[41] People might want dates for all of these plays, movies, and cruises, so they might well take advantage of the new dating services—904 of them, according to the 2002 economic census, employing close to 4,300 people.[42]

What should I do with my life? It's not just a good question; it's a hard question. The preadult is stunned with possibility, a predicament unknown to most of the human race up until very recently. Humans are social creatures naturally inclined to adapt to cultural rules and maps. Yet preadults have no instruction manuals. In simpler economies, young people simply followed clearly marked pathways that led them to a trade or craft or wage labor, or, if they were very lucky, to professional jobs. A preadult, on the other hand, is like a Hitchcockian hero pushed off the bus at an unmarked crossroads in the middle of the desert. Which way to go? True, some knowledge jobs have a pretty obvious path, which may partly explain the continuing appeal of law school. To become a lawyer, you take the LSATs; apply to law school; get your degree; and with the help of your school's job placement office and networking from summer internships, you (up until very recently, at any rate) get a job. Constitutional law may be really hard, but any fool can understand the steps you take to become a lawyer. A lot of today's careers are more mysterious. How do you become a documentary filmmaker? A grant officer for an international aid foundation? An entrepreneur?

As if the choices and pathways were not mystifying enough, preadults know that there is nothing certain about the knowledge economy. The rumble of restructuring, downsizing, recessionary contraction, churning, and the whole process of what economists call creative destruction, provides the background noise during the preadult's career search. Even before the current recession, some white-collar jobs were looking like the next targets for automating and offshoring. The possible victims include software and computer chip designers, engineers, insurance claim processors, and financial and legal analysts. A 2007 report from the consulting firm Booz Allen warns that American companies will be moving good jobs to China, India, or Brazil, not just to save money as we've seen in the past, but to seek out intellectual capital wherever they can find it.[43] Add to those worries reminders that people who start their careers during bad economic times see lifelong impacts on their earnings, and you get an epidemic of preadult insomnia.[44]

The bewilderment and anxiety of the graduate without a script has not escaped the notice of many people eager to help. Advice books with such titles as *Get It Together, I Don't Know What I Want But I Know It's Not This,* and *Plugged In: A Gen Y Guide to Thriving at Work* are now available to guide the preadult into the knowledge economy. There are scores of blogs, such as Graduated andclueless.com; Lifeaftercollege.org (motto: "No one said it was easy"); Ramenrentrésumés.com; Gradspot.com; and Thelemon life.com for the young grad's perusal. Some, such as Monster.com or Jobs.com, are simply lists of openings, much like pre-Internet newspaper classifieds; others are more specialized, focusing, for instance, on "millennial-friendly employers." Other websites, such as the popular BrazenCareerist.com, are multiservice destinations, providing practical advice, social networking, and articles in upbeat management-speak ("10 Ways Gen Y Will Change the Workplace") for the young wannajob. In May 2007, a young writer named Nadira Hira published an article in *Fortune* called "Attracting the Twentysomething Worker," and a career was born;

she became the magazine's millennial beat reporter and blogger advising newcomers to the job market and employers puzzling over a new generation of workers. Preadults who want some personal attention—and can afford it—might hire career experts or, more specifically, self-anointed "Gen Y career consultants" who offer personal video-coaching and Twitter updates. Come to think of it, they could just *become* Gen Y career consultants, another job no one had ever heard of before circa 2000.

Now, it is true that many grads don't need guidebooks, websites, or consultants. They have known what they wanted to do with their lives from the time they were handed their first Lego set or kiddie cookbook. This is especially the case for graduates in what is known as the STEM fields (science, technology, engineering, and math). Unlike most college kids, who change majors as often as roommates, STEM types tend to figure things out early on in their college careers or even in high school, and the large majority stick with their decisions.[45] That's not the way it goes for your typical English or government major. Those kids are in search mode. It's not as if a 22-year-old just knows she wants to be a university Title IX compliance manager or a foundation grant officer; the job description is too abstract, the required skills too diffuse. With the exception of professions requiring very specific talents like mathematics, music, and cooking, Peter Drucker explained in the *Harvard Business Review* in 2005, "Most people, especially highly gifted people, do not really know where they belong until they are well past their mid-twenties."[46]

No wonder that a lot of preadults paddle around the edges of this roiling economy before diving in. While they're pondering—or putting off—their options, they often go through a series of McJobs, as Douglas Coupland cleverly termed them in his 1991 hit *Generation X*, a book whose characters might be described as early-stage preadults. "I worked as a DJ; I worked in a bakery; I worked at a grocery store; I worked for a cleaner; I worked at a plant that made air filtration products," says one peripatetic 24-year-old interviewed by Jeffrey Arnett.[47] If they can figure out how to pay for it, some preadults trek through South America or China. Or they follow a childhood dream. Why not try to make it as an actor or painter? You don't have much to lose these days if you're 26 when you realize you aren't going to be the next De Niro or Koons. Ironically, the Great Recession may even have encouraged more risk and entrepreneurialism. "Necessity entrepreneurship" is a normal consequence of a weak economy, says *National Journal*, especially among millennials who were already an independent bunch. "[Millennials] are more aware that they're out alone and aware of the need to fend for themselves," the article quotes Bruce Tulgan, author of *Not Everyone Gets a Trophy: How to Manage Generation Y*, as saying. "The Gen-Y mind-set is not being stopped in its tracks by the recession. It's being reinforced."[48]

Others just try something, *anything*. Everyone has heard the truism that globalization, downsizing, restructuring, and intense competition have devoured the old-fashioned "company man," and that the predictable and stable job paths of the 1950s and 1960s have become as hard to find as a ribbon for a Smith Corona typewriter. Preadults have to be willing to move to find opportunity, particularly now, when unemployment varies so much from city to city. "Footloose young people are often in the best position to take advantage of these disparities by moving where the jobs are—or at least planning aggressive job-seeking visits," notes another article in *National Journal*.[49]

But it's also the case that young workers entering the crowded bazaar of the knowledge economy aren't necessarily looking for stability. They want to graze its offerings. Young workers have always been more mobile than the rest of the population. But the preadult has turned job change into a lifestyle. Approximately 35 percent of 20- to 29-year-olds have been working at their present jobs for less than a year; in their thirties, the number is still at 18 percent. Younger adults in their twenties have always "churned" through jobs, as the economists put it, more than older workers. Now, churning continues increasingly into the thirties.[50] With luck, churning can be a great strategy. *Dilbert* creator Scott Adams describes meeting one such preadult: "Last night I met a script supervisor. She works with directors to make sure a movie has the right continuity, and one scene fits the next. It's a fascinating job, hobnobbing with top directors, writers, and celebrities. No two assignments are the same. How do you get that kind of career? She earned a degree in anthropology and just 'fell into it' through a series of events." Adams, though considerably longer of tooth than preadults, has his own story in that vein. "I majored in economics, got an MBA, worked at a bank, then a phone company, and became a cartoonist."[51]

Another reason for the drawn-out career search is that preadults are looking for something much bigger than a way of earning a living. They are searching for meaning, for purpose, for a life mission, all of which, for good and not-so-good reasons, they believe should take the shape of a career. Amy and Leon Kass, professors at University of Chicago, used to ask their students, "What is the most important decision you will make in your life?" The answer was almost always "My career" or "What grad school to go to." When one student answered, "The mother of my children," he was greeted with hilarity from his classmates.[52]

In fact, it's probably not much of a stretch to say that the career search has become preadults' primary romantic quest, considerably more consuming and miles more deliberate than the hunt for a husband or wife, at least through much of their twenties. The language of romance pervades career talk. Preadults are far more likely to talk about "my dream job" than "the man [or woman] of my dreams." The word "passion" flows like Ritalin at exam time. "How Do I Find My Passion?" Gen Y career consultant Christine Hassler asks in an article on the website *Huffington Post*. Alexandra Levit, another in Hassler's line of work, offers a quiz that will reveal your "passion profile."[53] "Do what you love," goes a BlackBerry commercial showing a group of happy, texting preadults that's on television these days. "Love what you do."[54]

Nor is it just the artist or inventor who expects to be starry-eyed. The energy and give-it-your-all enthusiasm of the start-up continues to be the sentimental model for young career-seekers, even those in fairly traditional fields and even a decade after the dot-com bust. "I discovered a passion and aptitude for teaching preschool children," explains a 25-year-old in an interview in one popular book about twentysomethings. "I believe it to be the single most fascinating, emotionally rewarding, intellectually stimulating, and worthwhile profession there is."[55] In the past, someone—almost always a woman—taught preschool because the job had good hours, because it was relatively undemanding, and because kids were cute and fun. Now it's because she has found love. "Do what you love and the money will follow," goes one widely repeated, though dubiously optimistic, phrase sometimes bandied about by consultants and coaches.

Such a mindset would have struck most human beings in the past—and no doubt a sizable number today—as laughable. You tilled the ground, slopped the pigs, or placed a widget in a thingamajig because that's what you had to do if your family was going to eat. As legions of parents have reminded their kids, it wasn't called "work" because it was supposed to be fun. Work might be able to fund a passion, but it didn't arouse it. That way of thinking won't go far with this generation. "Our parents raised us to think we could do anything—and as a result, we're determined to have exactly our dream jobs," the Gen Y consultant Chris Borgan has announced. These sentiments have given rise to an impressive list of management books attempting to explain millennials to prospective employers and to address complaints that younger workers expect far too much in the way of entertainment and head-patting: for example, *Motivating the "What's in It for Me?" Workforce* and *Employing Generation Why*, as well as the less-judgmental *Managing Gen Y* and *Millennials Incorporated*. "This is the most high-maintenance workforce in the history of the world," Tulgan told *Fortune* magazine.[56] It's become close to conventional wisdom in some quarters that the problem goes beyond attitudes toward work. Gen Y, some say, suffers from an epidemic of narcissism.[57]

There may well be something to these plaints. Still, preadults are not crazy to expect more gratification from work than past generations could, even if they need to downgrade their expectations in the current environment. Karl Marx believed that industrial laborers suffered from "alienation" because they could not own either the means of production or the products they made themselves. Today's knowledge worker is the opposite of alienated. She owns her means of production; it's her brain, better known in economist-speak as "human capital." Being a fund-raiser for a museum or a scientist examining mouse cells requires more thought, problem-solving, and, yes, even creativity than rote work required in factories or in Scranton, Pennsylvania, paper company offices. The people person, the nurturer, the nature lover, the kid who planned the class parties, the sports nut, the food fanatic, the fashion crazed—as well as the person who loves four-year-olds—may well be able to find jobs to satisfy their inclinations. "Your calling is calling," promises Monster.com on its home page.[58] It's a good thing, too, because as the knowledge economy grew in the 1980s, so did the number of hours worked by college-educated workers—or men, at any rate.[59]

Obviously, preadults also want to make money. No one can live on love alone. In fact, on college surveys, millennials come across as more materialistic than their boomer parents. According to the American College Freshman survey, the percentage of college students to cite "being very well-off financially" as a top goal is the highest ever; college students of their parents' era were more likely to check off a "meaningful philosophy of life" as their chief aspiration.[60] But there is also no question that preadults do not equate career success with a big paycheck. Work is much too personal for that. They know that almost as soon as they meet someone, they will be asked, "What do you do?" The answer will be worth a thousand Facebook pictures. *Me 2.0* and *Do What You Are* are the sorts of career advice books they might read. Po Bronson found during interviews for his best seller that people would rarely talk about their work without interweaving some of their personal history, explaining the family and school experiences or talents and interests that should be part of any job.[61] You're not just looking for a job; you're expressing who you are, your talent, your passion.

"What should I do with my life?" then turns out to be another way of asking "Who am I?" Should the bum job market continue for very long, the conditions for optimistic preadulthood will fade. Young people could be forced to downsize dreams and to give up on, or at least drastically reduce, that decade of self-exploration. For the moment, however, the preadult still struggles with identity, not just a downsized paycheck. This is the meaning of the "quarterlife crisis," a popular phrase introduced in a 2001 book of that name by Alexandra Robbins and Abby Wilner.[62] Robbins and Wilner adapt their neologism from the familiar "midlife crisis," but their analogy is not quite right. The crisis they describe in their book is closer to Erik Erikson, the preeminent mid-century psychologist of adolescence, than Updike. The quarterlifer is the alienated youth dreaming of personal authenticity and "passion" in a world that threatens Dilbert-style misery for those unable to navigate the possibilities of the knowledge economy.

Adding to the crisis is the quarterlifer's anxiety that some of his peers are doing just fine. Better than fine, actually. Every 24-year-old can recite the dorm-to-riches stories: such student-entrepreneurs as Mark Zuckerberg, founder of Facebook, and Google creators Sergey Brin and Larry Page, who at 25 had indexed 26 million web pages and were hosting a half-million searches a day. Websites and magazines about these stars and many lesser strivers with their own impressive stories seem to mock the ordinary preadult. Ben Casnocha, who describes his own adventure founding a company when he was in middle school (!) in his book My Start-Up Life, has written on his blog:

> Today, if you're 24 and online, your sense of what's possible from a how-to-live-life perspective is limited by the bounds of a boundless internet. Sure, when you read newspapers from all over the world or follow blogs from people doing amazing things your arc of vision is broader than whatever is happening on your cul-de-sac. But this also means you can compare yourself, in vivid detail and in real-time, to whomever is at the top of the game you happen to be playing in. Possible consequence: feelings of inferiority, envy, slowness

(there's always someone younger who's done more and read more), stupidness, loneliness ("Everyone has it figured out but me").[63]

In high school, this generation of strivers had to build their résumés for college, they knew which clubs and teams they could join, the tests and papers all had a due date, and their parents could drive them wherever they needed to go. In college, it wasn't so different. They measured out their lives in exams, papers, sports events, and spring breaks. Suddenly, they're on their own with no teachers telling them what will be on the exam. There is no more template, as the website Untemplater implies in its name. "When I graduated from college, I received my diploma, walked off the stage and felt the weight of a completely unknown future," one young blogger writes. "It was the last act where I knew my lines. It was all ad lib from that point on. No one was providing the script anymore and I needed some lines. Where were those easy scripts? What were my next lines? At that moment, it had finally occurred to me that I should be planning something, or maybe should have already planned something . . . but what?"[64]

What indeed? Grad school? That means tuition bills and no income. Becoming a Starbucks barista? That's no plan; that's a delaying tactic. A real job (assuming any are available) in a field that offers "potential to grow"? For the preadult, career dominates future planning. The young careerist has to be able to move easily between school and internships, between internships and jobs, and between jobs in home cities and abroad. He may have to work fifty or sixty hours a week or more. According to the Families and Work Institute, almost 75 percent of 25- to 32-year-olds work more than forty hours per week, compared to 55 percent in 1977. Because they have the most up-to-date skills, says Richard Florida,

"Young recent graduates are the work horses of many sectors of the Creative Economy"; they have to "frontload" their careers.[65]

Under the circumstances, one thing the young grad is not going to plan is a wedding. And children? No way. Spouses and children are a ball-and-chain on the mobility required along the early knowledge-career track. For this reason above all, preadults marry later than ever before in history. In 1960, the average age of marriage for women was 20 and for men, 22. Today, for the total population, the median age of first marriage is 26 for women and 28 for men. Those with a college degree are even slower to tie the knot. College-educated women marry closer to 28, and those with graduate training have a median age of marriage between 29 and 30.[66] In parts of the Northeast and Middle Atlantic states—New York, New Jersey, Massachusetts, Rhode Island, and Washington, DC, where the percentage of college-educated people is particularly high—half of ever-married men didn't marry until they were past 30.[67]

And so, in the era of the preadult, becoming a grown-up is a far more ambiguous proposition than it has been at any point in the past. Are you an adult when you move out of your parents' house? At law school graduation? When you take the first job that limits jeans to casual Fridays? When you ask young people today what will make them adults, almost no one mentions marriage. They are far more likely to see issues around work—completing education, financial independence, a full-time job—as the signs that they have arrived.[68] Work, career, independence: these are the primary sources of identity today.

By contrast, consider some of the few other cultures where marriage occurred on the late side: specifically Western Europe in the early modern period and the United States in the eighteenth and nineteenth centuries. Until they married in their mid-twenties—marriage in the teens and early twenties was commonplace only in the 1950s and early 1960s—single folks remained part of the family economy, laboring in their parents' shops or farms, or at the very least, contributing to the family kitty. You might have been single at 24 in, say, 1900 when the median age of marriage in the United States was 26 for men, but you weren't living in a bachelor pad, much less an animal house. Fewer than 5 percent of unmarried people in their twenties headed their own households in 1900. Those who left home took a room in a boarding house and sent some of their meager wages to their families.[69] They ate with the families with whom they lodged. There was no singles scene, no condos or rental apartments with separate bedrooms and kitchens and bathrooms. Today in much of Europe and Asia, even though young people are marrying later, they also tend to live with their families, meaning that they continue to move straight from their parents' home to the home they share with a spouse.[70]

The movie *Failure to Launch* and a slew of media stories showing that this generation no sooner graduates from college than it flops down on the couch in front of their parents' television creates the impression that American preadults share these family values. Since the recession began, the theme has become even more pervasive. "By the middle of the aughts . . . the percentage of 26-year-olds living with their parents reached 20 percent, nearly double what it was in 1970," asserts one article in a typical mode.[71] It's true that there was a small uptick in the past decade in the percentage of people in their early twenties living in their parents' homes, a number that has risen, perhaps temporarily, during these bad economic times.[72] Some of that might be explained by immigration; second-generation immigrants tend to live at home as preadults.[73] For others, middle-class parents are the safety net while twentysomethings start their high-wire walk through the knowledge economy. Jason Ryan Dorsey, the 28-year-old author of *My Reality Check Bounced!*, puts it this way: "If we don't like a job, we quit, because the worst thing that can happen is that we move back home. There's no stigma, and many of us grew up with both parents working, so our moms would love nothing more than to cook our favorite meatloaf." Others, the subject of many media stories, are down on their luck, with no prospects in sight.

Yet, the failure-to-launch meme is highly misleading. The major trend of the past decades has been for the young not to depend more on family but rather to have greater autonomy and independence.[74] Many of the kids moving back home would have been in their own place with a spouse in 1970. The rest of them are living by themselves or with roommates. As the sociologist Michael Rosenfeld has shown, between 1960 and today, there was a small increase in the percentage of people between 25 and 29 living with their parents, but a much larger rise in the percentage of young living on their own.[75] When the Pew Center for Research reported that 10 percent of 18- to 34-year-olds had to move back in with their parents because of the economy, the media failed to notice that the number was lower than the 12 percent of preadults who decided to save money by finding roommates.[76] Condo developers in cities all over the country continue to advertise the single life, hinting at friendships, networking, and sex, a Melrose Place for the twenty-first century.[77]

The separation from family life takes us back to the singles television shows of the 1990s, the decade that saw the full emergence of the preadult. Shows such as *Friends* and *Seinfeld* promised compensation for the isolation of preadulthood. Friends substitute for the family you are too old to return to and the family you are too young to start.[78] They listen to your complaints about the boss or last night's date. They buy you shots on your birthday. They share Thanksgiving turkey with you. "Your job's a joke, you're broke, / Your love life's D.O.A. / It's like you're always stuck in second gear . . . I'll be there for you," go the lyrics to the theme song of the wildly popular sitcom that made Jennifer Aniston the perennial US Weekly cover girl.

At 41, Aniston is an ambivalent symbol of the hyper-successful single woman, now approaching middle age. Is she "Fabulous at 40!" as the headlines put it or, unmarried and childless, still treading the troubling waters of preadulthood? That's the thing about preadults. It's sometimes hard to know.

two

THE NEW GIRL ORDER

Sooner or later the world will get tired of *Sex and the City*, but it probably won't be anytime soon. That maxim holds despite the disastrous critical reception of the second movie in its name. After running on HBO for six years—from 1998 to 2004—the series remains on air in syndication in the United States as well as throughout Western Europe, the Czech Republic, Hungary, Poland, Israel, Brazil, Turkey (Turkey?!), South Korea, Slovenia, and the Ukraine. In the Middle East, those who can tune in from satellite television. The Chinese government censors the show, but pirated DVDs are enormously popular, even though they go under the lame title *Desire in the City*.[1]

Everyone knows why the show is so popular: sex, glamour, and wit. It's a universally irresistible formula. Less noticed is another striking attraction of the series: it has the most highly educated, professional characters of any situation comedy in television history. Indeed, I'd guess it has the most highly educated, professional characters of any cultural product anywhere, anytime, with the possible exception of such legal dramas as *The Good Wife* or campus novels by the likes of David Lodge. Consider the jobs of the heroines of *Sex and the City:* a lawyer (Harvard JD), a journalist, a public relations executive, and an art gallery manager (Smith BA). Every one of these strivers is a woman, every one a woman whose glamour is defined as much by her career as by her Manolos.

True, *Sex and the City* is "just a television show," and a fantastically mythical one at that. The series traded in overripe fantasies about the sweetness of female friendship, as well as about how many $400 shoes you could enjoy on a journalist's salary. Yet it is a momentous cultural document nonetheless, largely because it captures a fundamental truth about the new stage of preadulthood that came into its final shape in the 1990s: girls rule.

Notice I'm talking about preadult women, not their older sisters, mothers, or grandmothers. College-educated women of middle age, for instance, still tend to be a rare breed in corporate boardrooms, in the partner offices at law firms, and in the higher echelons of the financial world. (That's the apparent source of Mr. Big's riches, though this is the only topic about which *Sex and the City* writers were coy. More on this point in Chapter 6.) Women often feel like outsiders in these and other male enclaves; this is an especially common complaint about the computer industry. Women make up a small percentage of the United States Congress. When they run for office—or at least for president—people seem as interested in their hair, clothes, and cleavage as in their plans for the country. And yes, on average—a highly misleading average but an average nonetheless—they earn considerably less money than men.[2]

None of this belies the social and economic domination of today's young, college-educated women. Some of the relevant numbers may be familiar, some less so. But put together, they help define the novel ecosystem of preadulthood.

O Women between the ages of 25 and 34 with a bachelor's degree or higher outnumber men. This has been the situation since the 1980s, and the trends continue to be in women's favor. Between 1975 and 2006, the percentage of women with at least a college degree increased from 18.6 to 34.2 percent. Men barely budged: their numbers went from 26.8 percent to 27.9.[3] By 1980, most of the students in cap and gown at college graduation ceremonies were women. In 2004, the fair sex constituted 57 percent of graduating collegians. Today, it is 58 percent, and predictions are that women will reach 60 percent of the college grads in the near future.[4] Approximately 30-some percent of women between the ages of 25 and 34 have a bachelor's degree or higher, compared with 26 percent of their male peers.

Women are not just getting their parchment from Podunk U. They have joined, and in many cases, taken over, the country's elite schools. They rule at such prestigious state universities as the University of North Carolina, SUNY, and the University of California. True, engineering and tech schools remain predominantly male; Caltech, for instance, is 70 percent male. And at the oldest and preppiest of the preppy institutions—Yale, Princeton, and Dartmouth—men continue to outnumber women, though just barely. By the class of 2008, however, the fair sex dominated at Harvard;[5] they've ruled for years at Brown, the University of Pennsylvania, and Columbia. There are more women than men at high-ranking historically male schools, such as Amherst, Williams, Bowdoin, Tufts, and Haverford, not to mention the now-coed schools once graced only by women, such as Vassar, Sarah Lawrence, Bennington, and Skidmore. Meanwhile, women still have the high-status Bryn Mawr, Wellesley, Smith, Barnard, and Mount Holyoke pretty much to themselves.[6]

The formerly mostly male schools of the high establishment are hardly being chivalrous or politically correct in welcoming so many female students. Women are taking over because they have the right stuff. They are more likely to aspire to go to college than men.[7] As high schoolers, they're considerably more likely to take the SAT than their male counterparts. Women also make up the bulk of AP exam takers.[8] They have higher high school grades. According to the College Board, which administers the SAT college entrance exams in the United States, the average SAT-taking girl who graduated from high school in 2007 had a grade point average of 3.40, compared with the average boy's 3.24.[9] Yes, girls lag on their math SATs, a gap that has persisted since the College Board invented the hallowed exam. Still, although Barbie hated math, the new Bratz generation is game; they earn higher grades in math courses than do this cohort of Kens.

As for other parts of the college résumé, women are also on top. Go to a high school graduation; you'll notice that when it comes to the class president, the valedictorian, the achievement awards, and honor societies, it's girls, girls, girls. The National Center for Education Statistics recently asked tenth-graders about their educational expectations; 42 percent of girls said they planned to pursue a graduate or professional degree, compared with 29 percent of boys.[10]

The gender gap is now big enough that some college admissions departments are rumored to be resorting to preferences—sometimes referred to as affirmative action—to ensure that women don't take over the place, a charge that Office of Civil Rights officials are investigating.[11] (For reasons that probably have little to do with academics, most women—men for that matter, too—don't want to go to college where the opposite sex is scarce.[12]) Girl dominance is particularly a problem for smaller institutions that don't have largely male engineering schools to increase the population of guys. The College of William and Mary, for instance, has a 43 percent admittance rate for men and a 29 percent rate for women.

"We're the College of William and Mary, not the College of Mary and Mary," the admissions director once explained about the obvious advantage given to male applicants.[13]

O Once they are in college, women work harder and outperform men. Women college students spend more time studying and reading than their male counterparts. According to some studies, they contribute more to class discussion and have more frequent communication with faculty, including discussions about career plans. They volunteer more, they go to more arts events, and with the exception of intramural sports, they are more likely to participate in extracurricular activities.[14] Female college students are also nearly twice as likely to have studied abroad.[15] At least one study suggests that when they go abroad, female students gain more in terms of language and "intercultural sensitivity." (Male students actually *lost* ground in the latter, compared with a control group that didn't venture beyond their home campuses.)[16] Overall, men are less engaged in campus life, and they are less likely to take part in campus groups.[17] Richard Whitmire, author of *Why Boys Fail*, who has done intensive interviews with college professors and administrators, reports that one crucial difference between male and female students "is that men tend to be loners. The women would eagerly join study groups, which doubled as support groups, while the men went their own way."[18] Not surprisingly, women also graduate college with higher grade point averages than men.

Women are also successfully storming majors in formerly "male" terrain. In 1970, women constituted less than 10 percent of bachelor's degrees in business; today, it's more than 50 percent. Since that time, there has been a disproportionately large increase in the share of degrees in life sciences, physical sciences, and engineering earned by women.[19] Their grades are now higher than men's in math and science—and just about every other major.[20] Here's a commonplace observation from a professor from a northeastern university: "The men come into class with their backward baseball caps and the 'word processor ate my homework' excuses. Meanwhile, the women are checking their day planners and asking for recommendations for law school."[21]

O After they graduate, young women stay on the fast track. In the professions, their progress has been phenomenal. In 1960, women made up 6 percent of doctors and 3 percent of lawyers; today, those numbers are 49 percent and 47 percent, respectively. Some projections have it that they will be 70 percent and 60 percent, respectively, of those populations by 2050.[22] Overall, one hundred thirty-nine 25- to 29-year-old women hold advanced degrees for every one hundred men of the same age group.

In 2007, women earned 60 percent of master's degrees. As of 2008, they were getting more than 50 percent of all PhDs, a jump of more than ten percentage points since 1997.[23] Between 1997 and 2007, there was a 4 percent increase in the number of doctoral degrees for women, as compared with 1 percent for men. Between 1997 and 2007, the number of male full-time graduate students increased by 32 percent, compared to a 63 percent increase for female graduate students. Among part-time graduate students, the number of men increased by 10 percent, and the number of women increased by 23 percent.[24] On the graduate level, too, it's gotten so that in some academic fields, administrators have to scramble for male students. Here's a familiar sort of story told by *Reason* science writer Ronald Bailey:

A few years back, a friend who teaches in a graduate political science department at a prominent university told me that the women who applied to his school's program were so much more qualified than the male applicants that if all applicants were selected solely on the basis of academic merit, no men would be admitted to the program. That would be fine with my friend except for the fact that highly qualified women will not attend a program that is all female. Thus this program actually engaged in what amounts to affirmative action for males in order to attract and keep highly qualified female students.

There are a few exceptions to the female sovereignty over postgraduate education. Business schools remain predominantly male; at the top B-schools, women constitute between 30 and 40 percent.[25] Still, the trends are in women's favor. Since 2005, women's MBA enrollment has increased by 13 percent, according to a 2008 study by the Forte Foundation, a consortium of schools working to increase the number of women pursuing MBAs.[26] And young women are more likely to be starting businesses, an activity that arguably requires more drive and executive skills than filling out an application for grad school.

O Preadult women are now earning more than men. In New York, women between 21 and 30 make 117 percent of what their male peers make; in Dallas, the number is 120 percent. Several years ago, one study reported that young, college-educated women were earning more than men in Los Angeles, Chicago, Boston, and Minneapolis.[27] A newer study has expanded on the news; unmarried, childless women are outearning men in 147 of the 150 largest U.S. cities, and although the study is not limited to college-educated workers, the researchers see the trend at work in cities with larger knowledge economies.[28] What makes this new gender gap even more striking is that women choose college majors in fields that pay less than those majors chosen by men. Women constitute 79 percent of education majors and 71 percent of psychology majors; they are only 18 percent of higher-paying engineering and computer science majors.[29] When women go to business school, they take fewer of the finance courses that tend to lead to higher-paid positions.[30] College-educated women are more likely to work in the nonprofit sector and in local government, both less lucrative than for-profit and federal government jobs.[31] And yet, with all of those things working against them, they are still starting to outearn men.

O Young single women are more likely to own real estate than their guy peers. The National Association of Realtors reports that in the United States in 2005, single women made up 21 percent of the real estate market, compared with a paltry 10 percent for single men; the median age for first-time female buyers was 32.[32] The real estate firm Coldwell Banker has been making eyes at these young female buyers with a new motto, "Your perfect partner since 1906," while Lowe's, the home renovating giant, is offering classes especially for them.

Interestingly—and for reasons that will make more sense in the next chapter—female success is an international affair. In European countries, including Denmark, France, and Finland, more than half of all women between 20 and 24 are in school. The majority of college students are female in the United Kingdom, France, Germany, Norway, and Australia, to name only a few of many places.[33] The gender gap is quickly narrowing in more traditional countries, such as Korea, China, and Japan, where an increasing number of women in their twenties are part of the higher-education system. The number of countries where women constitute the majority of postgraduate degree candidates is also growing rapidly. In Japan, until recently one of the more traditional of developed societies, women entrepreneurs have been opening new businesses at twice the rate of men.[34]

With more women going to college and grad school, the age of marriage has soared in those countries, just as it has in the United States. The typical Spanish, French, Scandinavian, Irish, Japanese, or Korean woman is in her late twenties when she first ties the knot.[35] This transformation took about a generation to unfold in the United States; in Asia and Eastern Europe, it has been much more abrupt. In Korea, the percentage of single 30- to 34-year-old women doubled in just five years, going from 10 percent in 2000 to 20 percent in 2005.[36] In Spain, not so long ago a Catholic country where an unmarried girl was jealously chaperoned until the family handed her over to her husband at 21 or so, the percentage of women in higher education has increased by 40 percent during the same years that the average age of first giving birth has risen to near 30—probably a world record for any society in human history.[37]

Just as in the United States, young single women in Europe and Asia are pouring into urban centers in pursuit of career opportunities consistent with their educational pedigree. So many female strivers have moved out of villages and towns in eastern Germany to cities where the best jobs are that the Germans have coined a term—*frauenmangel*—to describe the trend. Catering to the new SYFs—single young females in demographer talk—has transformed city neighborhoods in Asia, Europe, and the United States. They sport a Manhattan singles vibe with a lot of bars serving cosmopolitans and other sweet cocktails, day spas, and boutiques selling designer jeans and bags. Few SYFs can afford their own apartments in such Asian cities as Shanghai or Tokyo, but they nevertheless aspire toward independence and a glam lifestyle à la

Sex and the City. Consider 37-year-old Li Yuan, now a writer at the *Wall Street Journal*.

> I first saw [*Sex and the City*] when I was living in Bangkok in 2000. I felt liberated. I was facing choices in both my career and my life, and learned from the show that I should make decisions based on how I wanted to live my life, and not on how other people wanted me to live my life.
>
> I can't afford Manolo Blahniks but I do have many pairs of shoes—too many for anybody visiting my small Brooklyn apartment. I don't feel the pressures to settle down, get married and have kids that a woman in her mid-30s would face in China. Nobody has told me—yet—that I'm weird. Above all, I don't feel guilty about enjoying my life. I'm proud of my choices, just like the characters in the show are. And I know my parents are proud of me too.[38]

This is what I call the New Girl Order.[39] For the first time ever, and I do mean ever, young women are reaching their twenties with more achievements, more education, more property, and, arguably, more ambition than their male counterparts. Throughout human existence, men were the ones holding the jobs, the degrees, the money, the power, the independence, and the expectation for action on the public stage. Now men have met their match—in many respects, their superiors. How did such a revolution occur in the space of a half-century, a small minute in the time of human civilized existence?

People generally give two related answers to this question: the pill and feminism. Those explanations are correct as far as they go. When the pill came on the market in 1960, state laws kept the drug away from unmarried women who, presumably would—or should—have little use for it. Over the next fifteen years, however, one by one the states changed their age of consent laws, and by 1976, the pill was available to just about anyone who wanted it, including teenagers. That gradual legalization has provided social scientists with an interesting natural experiment about the pill's impact on young women's behavior. Comparing different localities, economist Martha Bailey was able to show that when a state changed its law, it saw a decline in the percentage of women giving birth by age 22. That state also experienced an increase in the number of women in their late twenties and early thirties who were in the labor force as well as in the number of hours they worked.[40] The pill clearly enabled more young women to join and stay in the workforce.[41] Today, and for the foreseeable future, it remains the leading form of contraception for women under 30.[42]

As for the second answer to the question of the origins of the New Girl Order—feminism—that also seems clear. Feminism encouraged achieving women to replace the so-called MRS. degree and domesticity with a new life plan. It celebrated the idea that women should seek fulfillment through work, apart from their roles as wives and mothers. It led activists to lobby for antidiscrimination laws. Equally important, it told women they could and should be financially independent of their husbands.[43]

Still, the pill was by no means a sufficient catalyst for the remarkable transformation from the "problem with no name" to *Sex and the City*. And neither it nor feminism was a guarantee of women's success in school or in the office. There's more to the story of women's success than that. In order to get a broader account of the foundations of the New Girl Order and to have a more complete sense of its extraordinary novelty, we need to tweak these explanations.

Let's start with the pill. For all of its profound impact, the pill was actually the culmination of a long series of inventions stretching back to at least the mid-nineteenth century that paved the way to the New Girl Order. For millennia—yes, thousands of years—if a female made it to her twenties, her life was defined by the reproductive imperative: pregnancy, childbearing, nursing, and feeding her young. In the United States from the 1880s until 1970—where we have the best numbers—the highest median age for marriage was 21.4 and first birth, 23.5, and that was during the Great Depression.[44] Some might think of this fate as proof of patriarchal oppression, but the real oppressor was Mother Nature. Nature made it so that there was no way to have sex and stop the babies from arriving. It also assured everyone, men and women, a life of drudgery. The vast majority of people in the Western world lived in conditions much like those in sub-Saharan Africa and parts of the Middle East today. Children were crucial helpers in the struggle to gather wood, farm the fields, hike to the well, or do piecework in the tenement room. Add to all of these hardships a life span that was likely to end somewhere between 40 and 50, and through most of history, women in their twenties had no choice but to be—crudely put—breeders and domestic laborers.

Even at the beginning of the twentieth century, a typical American woman was confined by nature's harsh laws. According to economists Stefania Albanesi and Claudia Olivetti, "She married at 21 and gave birth to more than three live children between age 23 and 33. The high fetal mortality rate implied an even greater number of pregnancies, so that she would be pregnant for 36 percent of this time."[45] Indeed, 30 percent of infants died before their first birthday.[46] The general rule was that women who had sex had babies, much the way that other mammals—indeed all animals—did.

It was only during the period that historians call the Second Industrial Revolution of the late nineteenth and early twentieth centuries that ordinary young women began to find release from nature's reproductive and subsistence-level demands. Without the huge technological advances of that period and without the market to provide these life-changing products at ever more affordable prices, women would still be tied to the home, pill or no pill. To put the point a little differently, nineteenth- and twentieth-century market capitalism built the foundations for the New Girl Order.

It would be an understatement to say that this is not the way most feminists have described female progress. More typically, feminist historians have described women as capitalism's slave class, whose unpaid domestic labor allowed the market's machinery to rumble on.[47] Actually, no. Unpaid domestic labor was a fact of life for women in all human civilizations—not to mention precivilizations. It was only with the mass affluence produced by technology and open markets that women could even think about earning a salary over years at a time, much less building a career. And, as we'll see in the next chapter, it was only advanced technology and complex economies that produced more of the kinds of careers women would be eager to pursue.

Consider one small moment during the mid-nineteenth century, a period of particularly rapid discovery and change. In the late 1830s, after years of obsessive tinkering and financial hardship, a small businessman by the name of Charles Goodyear discovered that by adding sulfur to India rubber he could increase its strength and flexibility. Goodyear patented the process, known as "vulcanization," and it was quickly used to make life preservers, shoes, and shirring for clothing, including fashionable ruffles for men's shirts. It also became an ideal material for contraceptive devices. Condoms had been around for centuries, of course, but made of animal intestines and unprocessed rubber, they were of poor quality—easily punctured, brittle in cold weather, and meltable in the summer. They were also expensive enough to be beyond the reach of most people. With vulcanization and better manufacturing processes, condoms and diaphragms, or "womb veils" as they were called at the time, not only became more reliable, they also became considerably cheaper. By the 1870s, working men and women could go to the pharmacy and pick up a dozen condoms for a dollar or two.

Though Goodyear's invention might seem relatively minor compared to the birth control pill, it undoubtedly helped young women escape their fate as "breeders." At the beginning of the nineteenth century, white women had an average of seven children—at least those who managed to live until menopause. To repeat: seven children, though not all of them lived, of course. By 1900, the number of children had almost been halved: 3.56. Most of that decline came about between 1840 and 1880, the years that cheaper contraception was reaching the mass market.[48] Birthrates continued to fall throughout the first half of the twentieth century until the end of the Depression. Compared to the pill, the condom had, and still has, its disadvantages. Condoms have a nasty tendency to break, they interfere with the mood of the moment, and—a minus from many a woman's point of view—they are controlled by men. But along with the diaphragm, they went a long way toward easing the reproductive imperative—at least for married women. As Gail Collins points out in her book *When Everything Changed: The Amazing Journey of American Women from 1960 to the Present*, pre-pill contraceptive advances were mostly helpful for women who wanted to limit their family size to two or three instead of five or six children; they were not reliable enough to keep a sexually active woman pregnancy-free over a significant period of time.[49] Nevertheless, the arrival of increasingly dependable birth control had a profound psychological and cultural effect. It began to release women from the fatalism that has been a default mental position for human beings throughout history. Women could plan their lives rather than giving themselves up to an "It's God's will" or "Nothin' I can do about it" mentality that suppresses human flourishing.

When it comes to market-driven progress easing the lives of women, improvement in birth control was only the beginning. Albanesi and Olivetti go on to describe the severe health risks that accompanied pregnancy and childbirth at the beginning of the twentieth century: septicemia, toxemia, hemorrhages, and obstructed labor "could lead to prolonged physical disability and, in the extreme, death."[50] A single, childless woman was not immune to these ailments. She would be expected to help mothers, aunts, or sisters—and their children—who suffered from their effects. These plagues only eased with the invention of antibiotics, blood banks, improvements in prenatal and obstetric care, and the mass production of safe baby formula, many the products of market innovation.

Ironically, for a time the same medical advances that improved mothers' health also added to women's domestic obligations, obligations that unmarried daughters would have been required to respect as well. The germ theory of disease that became part of medical thinking by the late nineteenth century dramatically reduced septicemia, the main cause of maternal death. By simply washing and disinfecting their hands before delivery, doctors and midwives learned to decrease the risk of this dreadful infection. But, the germ theory also increased mothers' work. It upped the demand for household cleanliness and more generally introduced the idea that "mothers could, by their actions, affect the life and well-being of their offspring."[51] Betty Friedan famously wrote in

1960 that "housewifery expands to fit the time available."[52] This may have been true in her own day, but in, say, 1910, before the arrival of labor-saving domestic technology, doctors had reason to believe that conscientious housewifery could save lives. And they were undoubtedly correct.[53]

In most other ways, however, science and technology were dramatically reducing the burdens of household labor. In 1900, few homes had electricity; only about a quarter of all households had running water. (This is still the case in rural China, as Leslie Chang describes in *Factory Girls*. There is very little electricity; no plumbing or heating; and workers wear gloves and coats inside, where families also store grain, raw pork, and cured fish hanging on hooks and where chicken scurry underfoot.[54]) In this environment, American women did what women—single and married— have always and everywhere done: cooking, making and cleaning clothes, hauling water, and the like. The "household revolution" of the early twentieth century reduced these burdens markedly. First came central heating, relieving families from the burdens of gathering wood and coal. Then there was indoor plumbing— running water and household toilets. And finally electricity, which eventually led to sewing machines, washing machines, refrigerators, electric irons, vacuum cleaners, and, in recent memory, microwaves.[55]

Consider Gail Collins's description of the labors of a young farm wife just trying to do the laundry: "She heated water on a wood-burning stove and washed the clothes in a tub, scrubbing the soiled pieces against a washboard to loosen the dirt. The clothes were then wrung by hand and hung outside on a line." After bringing the laundry inside—where in wintertime it would have to thaw—she wrestled with a clumsy and unreliable flatiron that she heated on the stove. A century ago? Actually, this was in the

1950s, a time when the mothers of some of today's preadults were children; in other words, a time remembered by some of us.[56] Scholars have concluded that the household revolution explains much of the increase of married women moving into the paid workforce toward the middle of the twentieth century when the early blessings of science and technology were not only available but were increasingly affordable.[57] As for younger singles, it made planning for a career more than a pipe dream. Notice that this was well before the arrival of second-wave feminism in the 1960s. (First-wave feminism refers to the suffragette movement of the second half of the nineteenth century.)

Nothing freed women more than progress in textile production. This story goes way back, beginning in the eighteenth century, when prefabricated cloth first came to the marketplace, but it continues to contemporary times. The mid-nineteenth century saw the invention of the sewing machine, and by the later years of the century, relatively inexpensive men's clothing was available. Ready-made clothing for women came along shortly after that.[58]

In 1950, clothing was still expensive enough that it took up 12 percent of average household expenditures; that's compared to 4 percent in 2007.[59] Before the days of Wal-Mart and Target, many families had to rely on hand-me-downs and handmade clothing. Several years ago, while flying from New York to North Carolina, I chatted with a black woman in her early sixties who was sitting next to me. Telling me about her children and grandchildren, she mentioned in passing that she used to make her children's clothes when they were little partly because she was good at it, but mostly to save money. She had been a nurse at the time, in the 1950s and 1960s, and her husband was a postal worker. I asked if her daughter, who was also a nurse, made clothes for her children. The answer, you will not be surprised to hear, was no. Before the Wal-Mart and

Target era, lower-middle-class women often made their own clothes, and not because they loved the DIY life. No, making clothes was crucial for controlling the household budget.

The point here is that by the mid-twentieth century, a woman reaching age 20 found herself living in an utterly reshaped habitat from that of her ancestresses, free from sepsis, unplanned children, caring for ailing sisters and aunts, sewing, bread-baking, and arduous trips to the river or well. By 1970, with the birth control pill available at a nearby pharmacy, she had reason to feel she had just about entirely fooled Mother Nature.[60] Second-wave feminism was in large measure a response to this new reality, a point that Betty Friedan well understood. "[M]ore and more of the jobs that used to be performed in the home have been taken away: canning, making bread, weaving cloth, making clothes" she wrote.[61] At the simplest level, middle-class women demanded a place at the table because they wanted more to do. But now that technologically based mass affluence made it feasible, they also wanted power and independence, including, if they so chose, independence from husbands. And so they did choose. The percentage of women in the labor force rose from 33 percent in 1948 to 59 percent in 1995, more or less where it stands today, with the most rapid growth occurring between 1975 and 1985.[62]

Women's march into the workplace was so complete that girls who would grow up to become preadults never knew a world where women didn't have jobs outside their homes. By 1980, the majority of them were growing up with working mothers.[63] No one had to tell them they would be working; it was as much a part of their life expectation as it was for their brothers. But middle-class parents had bigger plans for their girls than just a 9-to-5 job and a steady income. They wanted their girls to create a new breed.

Starting in the late 1970s and early 1980s, these aspirations led to a new sort of child—or more specifically girl—rearing that Barbara Dafoe Whitehead has called the Girl Project.[64] Boomer mothers and fathers made preparing their daughters for the world that their own generation had created their number-one domestic task. These girls would be powerful, confident, ambitious, and strong. No more "future wives and mothers" talk. No more relying on husbands as breadwinners. Sugar and spice? That was for the kitchen, a room in which these girls would not be spending much time (unless, of course, they wanted a career as a *chef de cuisine*). The gung-ho spirit of the Girl Project was captured by the Girl Scouts' new motto: "It's a girl's life. Lead it."

The Girl Project got its first boost a good decade before today's preadult women were born, when in 1972 Congress passed Title IX of the Education Amendments. Title IX outlawed discrimination against girls in any school receiving federal aid, and quickly enough, that was translated into a requirement to equalize school spending on sports for girls and boys. Title IX turned out to be a fantastically successful feat of social engineering. By the mid-1980s, team sports had become as obligatory a part of American girlhood as it had been for boys.

The schools were a big part of this transformation, but it was parents, particularly fathers, who translated Title IX into a middle-class lifestyle known as "soccer parenting." They loved having daughters who played sports, even if it did mean swim practice at 6:00 A.M. and basketball games until 7:00 P.M.; it sure beat jump rope and tea parties. Sports, they realized, promoted the strengths their girls would need to make it in a competitive marketplace:

discipline, courage, and a rivalrous spirit. Dan Kindlon, a Harvard psychologist who has written about coaching his daughter's softball team, describes how at first his athletes "shrieked hysterically" every time the ball came in their direction. Determined to "coach them like men," he announced that anyone who shrieked would be required to run laps. The noise stopped, and the girls were gradually transformed into eager and tough competitors.[65] As of 1971, women weren't allowed to run in the Boston Marathon; twenty years later, girls were collecting as many trophies as their brothers.[66]

In fact, the Girl Project was quickly and amazingly successful. By large margins, young women say it is very important that they be "economically set" before they consider getting married.[67] Psychologist Jean Twenge looked at 165 studies undertaken between 1931 and 1995 and found a steady rise in female assertiveness. During that time, women grew far more likely to value such stereotypically masculine traits as forcefulness, ambition, and self-reliance. In fact, by the early 1990s, college women were just as likely to be in-your-face as college men.[68] According to Twenge, female millennials easily out-assert their boomer mothers. Another study of middle school girls found a similar impatience with anyone acting "girly."[69] Kindlon labels "the new American girl" the alpha girl and in his own study discovered her to be "talented, highly motivated, and self-confident."[70]

Oddly, a lot of experts didn't notice the emergence of the alpha girl. Throughout the 1990s, academic and pop psychologists warned the public about an epidemic of passivity and low self-esteem among young women. The leader of the pack was Carol Gilligan, coauthor of the 1992 *Meeting at the Crossroads*, a book that started a revolution in female psychology. Gilligan argued that until they were about 7 or 8 years old, girls were at ease with themselves and projected "authentic voices." As they grew into adolescence, however, the adult world "silenced" them, subjecting them to "the tyranny of the nice and kind."[71] By 1994, *Meeting at the Crossroads* had a companion piece in Mary Pipher's best-selling *Reviving Ophelia: Saving the Selves of Adolescent Girls*, which described America's "girl-destroying" culture. There were many other books in the same vein: Myra and David Sadker's *Failing at Fairness: How America's Schools Cheat Girls*; Peggy Oren-stein's *Schoolgirls: Young Women, Self-Esteem, and the Confidence Gap*; Barbara Mackoff's *Growing a Girl: Seven Strategies for Raising a Strong, Spirited Daughter*; as well as a 1991 report from the American Association of University Women asking—and answering in the affirmative—"Are Our Schools Shortchanging Girls?" Marie C. Wilson, onetime president of the Ms. Foundation, and her coauthors of *Mother Daughter Revolution*, rallied women not "to leave their daughters adrift in a hostile world."[72]

Failing to recognize the signs that young women were already on academic and psychological steroids, legislators and policy-makers took their cue from the backward-looking experts. Girls needed more attention, more encouragement, and more ambition, they agreed. In 1993, Gloria Steinem with the Ms. Foundation launched Take Our Daughters to Work Day, intended as an annual attempt to introduce girls to the workplace that they were suppos-edly indifferent to. (Actually, in 1993, women constituted 45 per-cent of the labor force;[73] perhaps in recognition of the dubious reasoning behind the program, in 2003 it was quietly renamed Take Our Daughters and Sons to Work Day.) The year 1994 saw the passage of the Gender Equity in Education Act, which pro-vided extra funds for educators to help girls succeed. College schol-arships especially for girls sprouted up everywhere. Money poured in to help girls bring their math and science scores in line with those of boys. Meanwhile, textbook companies banned pictures of housewives and nurses from their pages and scanned history for heroic female role models. The project was successful enough that after looking over history textbooks of the time, education researcher Sandra Stotsky wrote—and not in jest—"Students may end up thinking that the West was settled chiefly by females, most often accompanied by their parents."[74]

Marketers quickly saw what was happening and gave the new zeitgeist a name. They called it girl power. Here were middle-class parents—in other words, doting mothers and fathers with discretionary income—looking for ways to bolster their daughters' self-esteem. Here were girls, typically more appearance-conscious than their brothers, who were being encouraged to "express themselves" and to believe, in the words of the title of a popular book, that *Girls Know Best*. If you're a marketer, what's not to love? Novelty companies started producing T-shirts saying "Girlmogul" and "Supergirl" as well as "Girls Are A-mazing" clocks, pillows, jewelry, magnets, journals, and backpacks. Marketing gurus began speaking of a new demographic: the tween. Female tweens were especially appealing to fashion and cosmetics companies, which appreciated the commercial possibilities of girl empowerment, including, to many parents' horror, thongs and other kinds of "stripper wear" for 11-year-olds. Most companies were more tasteful. Venerable Cleveland-based cosmetics firm Bonne Bell advertised its lip gloss with the words "I know I will succeed" next to a photo of a pretty young thing. The ad included a list with checkmarks next to each item: "I have a brain. I have lip gloss. I have a plan, I have a choice. I can change my mind. I am a girl."[75]

Also alert to the rise of girl power were television and movie producers. They brought a new kind of girl to the screen: self-confident, independent, smart, mouthy—and a kick-ass fighter.

These role models were supposed to revise the sentimental education of yesterday to show young girls destined to star on the soccer field, in physics class, and in writing briefs. As they were learning through Little League, no squealing, giggling, or "throwing like a girl" allowed. By elementary school, Disney-watching millennials could cast off *Cinderella* and *Snow White* in favor of the warrior girls *Pocahontas* and *Mulan*. In the mid-1990s, the campy *Xena: Warrior Princess* became the country's number-one syndicated show. A few years later, the Cartoon Network introduced *The Powerpuff Girls* (creator Craig McCracken originally called it "The Whoop-Ass Girls"), giving kindergarten femmes superpowers; it was a huge hit both on the small screen and in toys and accessories at Toys R Us. One of the most intriguing cultural products of the 1990s was the much-admired, girl-powered drama *Buffy the Vampire Slayer*.

The future citizens of the New Girl Order also had new grown-up role models on the big screen: the sweaty Ripley, played by an Amazon-like Sigourney Weaver, in *Aliens*; muscular Sarah Connor in *Terminator*; the spit-and-polished Demi Moore in *A Few Good Men*; and the police detective played by Jodie Foster in *Silence of the Lambs*. Meanwhile, the music world generated its own powerful girls: the Spice Girls, Madonna, and Alanis Morrisette, and for more indie types, Liz Phair and the Riot Grrl crowd, a boon to a music industry that could now claim an increasingly large consumer base. Girls' magazines also welcomed the empowered girl. They included *Sassy*, the brainchild of the forcefully hip Jane Pratt that debuted in 1988, and *YM*, a magazine that ran a section called "Girl Zone: Your Guide to Kicking Butt."[76] By the end of the 1990s and today as well, call a girl a "badass," and you are paying her the highest of compliments.[77]

Determined to have their daughters keep their eyes on the prize—The Big Career—some parents banished the word "marriage" from the young millennial vocabulary. Beautiful Bride Barbie? Not in our toy box, thank you very much. It was not unusual to hear of parents who warned their girls they would not be paying for any weddings before they reached 30. "No one, not my family or my teachers, ever said, 'Oh yes, and by the way you might want to be a wife and mother too.' They were so determined we would follow a new, egalitarian, modern path that the historic ambitions of generations of women—to get married and raise a family—were intentionally airbrushed from their vision of our future," writes one columnist for the *Times*.[78] Once upon a time, men might take their uninitiated sons to visit a prostitute. Now mothers took their girls to see *The Vagina Monologues* or to *Sex and the City* viewing parties to see what female sexual freedom and independence should look like. You can hear echoes of this education still. Women are quick to remind people that although they may like the idea of getting married, they don't actually *need* a husband, or even want one very much. In her lightning rod of a book *Marry Him*, fortysomething Lori Gottlieb lists some of the responses she got to an article about her regrets over not marrying: "I am totally appalled by your need for a man," "Get some self-esteem," and "If my daughter grows up to want a man half as much as you do, I will know I've done something wrong in raising her."[79] Descendants of girl power want it known that they are first and foremost capable, self-contained units. Career and independence required. Love, marriage, husbands, and children entirely optional.

A lot of people noticed that there were some downsides to girl power. Some asked whether girls were cracking under the strain of high expectations. They cited worrying rates of bulimia, anorexia, depression, and panic attacks among the high achievers. Girls Inc.'s contribution to the genre, based on a survey of more than 1,000 high school seniors, was a report titled "The Supergirl Dilemma: Girls Grapple with the Mounting Pressure of Expectations."[80] "For Girls, It's Be Yourself, and Be Perfect, Too," was the title of a 2007 article on the "amazing" girls of Newton, Massachussetts, in the *New York Times*. One girl described in the piece was "a great student, classical pianist, fluent in Spanish, and a three season varsity runner and track captain." Another, whose junior thesis for advanced placement history won Newton North's top prize, was an actress and president of her church youth group, as well as being in two advanced placement classes.[81] In articles such as these—and there are many of them—the words "overwhelmed," "pressure," and "anxiety" appear repeatedly.

But there is another, less-often-asked question: where do boys fit into the girl-powered world? It would be nice to be able to say that child-rearing is not a zero-sum game, that America loves all of its children equally. It would be nice. But even clueless boys might have noticed that by the 1990s, America had a favorite child, and the name of that child was Samantha, Megan, or Jessica. Money poured in for experts determined to bring girls' science and math scores up to par with boys'; as for boys' lower reading scores, well, it seemed Americans could live with that. "There's even a sense," including among the most privileged families, mused a 2003 *BusinessWeek* cover story, "that today's boys are a sort of payback generation—the one that has to compensate for the advantages given to males in the past."[82] There was the Women's College Coalition, which "makes the case for women's education to the higher education community, to policy makers, to the media and to the general public," but no Men's College Coalition anywhere to be found. Here's University of Michigan economist Mark J. Perry after chronicling the college and postcollegiate gender gap: "There are hundreds, if not thousands, of University and College Women's Centers across the country. . . . A Google search of 'College Women's Centers' finds almost 6,000 links on the Web. A Google search of 'College Men's Centers' finds almost no links on the Internet (fewer than 10), and asks the question: Did you mean: 'College *Women's* Centers'?"[83]

The success of young women came with an air of celebration and entitlement ("I can change my mind. I am a girl") and quite a few assertions of female superiority. "Girls Rule, Boys Drool," said the girls' T-shirts, posters, and skateboards. Watching television, boys—and men—were frequently reminded of their sex's genetic stupidity, insensitivity, and general cluelessness. There is Lisa Simpson, smart, studious, and sensitive. And then there is her brother Bart, "an underachiever and proud of it." On *Xena: Warrior Princess*, men were portrayed, in the words of one commentator, as "unreconstructed dirt and stubble-covered barbarians with matted hair and really bad teeth who travelled in packs torching everything in their path."[84] "Testosterone is a great equalizer," Buffy the vampire slayer's "watcher" tells her. "It turns all men into morons." *The Onion* once published a headline "Women Now Empowered by Everything a Woman Does." The editors might have also included: "Men Screw Up Everything a Man Tries."

Arguably, this is all in fun. Some of the most memorable comedy limns exaggerated stereotypes; we are often being asked to laugh at our own prejudices as much as at the tics of others. Or you could say that the culture of male privilege is so powerful that it can't hurt for boys to be pulled down a peg or two. But neither of those points should make anyone sit comfortably with the growing evidence that Americans now like girls better than boys.

In a 2009 article in *Elle*, Ruth Shalit Barett uncovered a new con-temporary trauma she calls "gender disappointment," suffered by mothers of sons who desperately want a daughter. According to Barett, for a lot of mothers, this "free-floating girl lust" doesn't go away even after they have had plenty of time to bond with their sons.[85] Boys just don't do it for them.

Barett's evidence is not merely anecdotal. Seventy-one percent of American families who use MicroSort—a company that claims to be able to sort sperm to increase your chance of getting the gen-der you want—want a daughter. "The era of wanting a first-born male is gone, not to return," Barett quotes founder Ronald Erics-son, MD, as saying. Girls "can do everything a boy can do, plus you can dress them up. It's almost like, to fit in, you need to have one." Adoptive parents in the United States also show a strong preference for girls.[86] Interestingly enough, whereas India and China continue to prefer boys, parents in former boy-bastions South Korea and Japan have also become partial to girls.[87]

Well, maybe boys have their issues with girl power. In the meantime, those strong and sassy girls are entering their preadult years a little anxious—it's not easy out there in the global knowl-edge economy—but pumped with excitement. It's a girl's life, and they are going to lead it! "The alpha girls we interviewed see themselves as unconstrained," writes Dan Kindlon. "Unfettered. They feel they have limitless choices. They are savvy enough to realize their sex may be an advantage rather than a disadvantage as they move into occupations that have formerly been domi-nated by men."[88]

All around the Internet, in movies, and in television shows, most notably *Sex and the City*, women of the New Girl Order pro-ject a giddy optimism and determined fabulosity. Check out *The Goddess Guide to Life: How to Be Absolutely Divine on a Daily Basis,* described as "a sassy and practical guide to the goddess you know you are." Or on the Internet, click onto DamselsinSuccess, Start upprincess, Corporette, Shetakesontheworld.com ("Create your career, live your dreams"), Joyfulbusiness, Divamarketing, Advancingwomen, or Theglasshammer (for glass ceilings). Or try Stratejoy, a networking and empowerment site for women: "Perhaps you're a corporate go-getter, or a kick ass mom, or a quarter lifer rockin' the city," chirps the website. "I get a Gen Y babe who refuses to settle for a 'good enough' life. You want the whole enchilada. You want the energy that comes along with being authentic, the 'I love my life' sparkle."

Career equals glamour, passion, and a life fully lived. Thank goddess there are careers out there that (sort of) live up to the hype. That is the subject of my next chapter.

three

PORTRAIT OF THE ARTIST AS A YOUNG BUSINESSWOMAN

In 1980, an artist by the name of Mark Vallen created a street poster that became a cover for *LA Weekly* and earned a few minutes of deserved fame. It showed a black and white cartoon drawing of a weeping woman, hand pressed in anguish against her forehead. "Nuclear War?!" the text reads. "There goes my career!"

Vallen appears to have meant the poster to protest the heightening of cold war hostilities at the time. But intentionally or not, his placard also poked fun at the feverish careerism that had seized women in the early days of second-wave feminism. We generally think of feminists urging women into the workplace to free them of their economic dependence on their husbands and their second-class status. Vallen's character's distress is a reminder that there was more to it than that. The activity of work itself was supposed to be liberating. Work—that is, paid work outside the home—was the opposite of mind-numbing domestic drudgery. It would stimulate women's minds, widen their narrow horizons, and let them take part in the basic human activity of invention and creation. "Vacuuming the living room floor—with or without makeup—is not work that takes enough thought or energy to challenge any woman's full capacity," Betty Friedan has written. "Down through the ages, man has known that he was set apart from other animals by his mind's power to have an idea, a vision, and shape the future to it . . . when he discovers and creates and shapes a future different from his past, he is a man, a human being."[1]

When you really think about it, there's one big problem with what Friedan is saying here. Down through the ages, most work failed to challenge women's *and* men's full capacities. Tied to caring and providing for their young, women may not have been in a position to "discover" and "create," but the truth is few men had that pleasure either. (A fall 2010 sitcom called *Raising Hope* evokes just this truth. A young laborer says to his mother, a cleaning woman, "There has to be more to life than cleaning the same pool over and over." She snaps back, "There isn't.") Work was largely about surviving in an inhospitable natural environment—obtaining food; building shelter; providing warmth; and protecting yourself from predators, animal and human. Remember the Genesis story of Adam and Eve's expulsion from the Garden of Eden? In paradise, the two enjoy leisure and ease. Banished to the real world, Adam has to "till the ground from whence he was taken." He works to survive. To be human meant to toil; work was the opposite of pleasure and ease. Lest you think this is ancient history, remember that as late as 1900, close to 40 percent of the U.S. labor force worked on farms. In much of the developing world, subsistence farming remains the norm.

Yet today, for a large swath of the developed world—and this is especially the case for women—the notion that work expresses our deeper identity is not at all odd. Young people believe that work can arouse passionate commitment the way it might have for, say, Vincent van Gogh or Ludwig van Beethoven. It should be a cognitive and emotional adventure, stimulating and rich in meaning. "Work. Life. Possibilities." goes a motto for Monster .com. We are all artists now—at least that's the plan.

There is no way fully to understand preadulthood or modern feminism without grasping this nexus of ideas. Yet they are ideas that would never be more than a toddler's fairy tale without a fundamental transformation of the economy over the past decades. The changed economy, which turns out to be very, very female friendly, is the very infrastructure for the New Girl Order. In the background of young women's success, then, there is the pill and there is feminism, as we saw in the previous chapter. There is also the knowledge economy.

Young women of the New Girl Order are not the first in history to move to the city to find work. More than a century ago, single young women in the United States worked at first mostly as domestics, though some were lucky enough to become dressmakers, salesgirls, and clerks. To modern ears, these jobs sound dreary, but for young women who had left their farms or small towns, the city offered excitement, freedom, and new sorts of consumer pleasure as well as a salary.

Factory Girls, a recent account of young female migrants in China by journalist Leslie Chang, gives an idea of what life must have been like for earlier generations of young working girls. In their mid- to late teens, these young women labor on miserable factory floors building electronics or shoes for ten-plus hours a day. They live in crowded dorms that, says Chang, always smell of wet laundry and offer no privacy, something that few of them have ever known anyway in the small, unheated homes of their villages. For all its Dickensian misery, city life seems preferable to their existence in muddy villages. The girls are able to save enough to buy a few consumer trinkets now and again and, equally important, to experience independence and a sense of possibility. They move from job to job, usually from one factory floor to the next, but sometimes they are lucky enough to land a supervisory or office position. "Her dream was to be a secretary in an office," Chang writes of one of her subjects.[2] Not much of a dream by our standards, but it's about as far as they can go. Most women will marry in their early twenties, "when [their] value is at its peak."[3]

In the United States, by the middle of the twentieth century, married women also moved into the workforce in large numbers. Though it's not the way we usually imagine the period, between 1950 and 1970 the percentage of married working women between ages 33 and 45 was already rising from to 25 to 46 percent. Most of those women were secretaries, waitresses, and clerks who would have sold their firstborn to endure the Westchester concentration camp hated by Friedan. The small percentage of women with an education had more satisfying opportunities; they became teachers, nurses, and librarians. Still, for the most part up until the 1970s, women looked for employment for the simple reason that they and their families needed the money.[4] Identity, meaning, passion: no one used words like that.

This is not to say that there weren't women who wanted to become scientists, doctors, lawyers, and the like, and that discrimination didn't keep them from doing so. There were many such women. In fact, sexism was a given, including in professional circles. In her history of post-1950s women, *When Everything Changed*, Gail Collins quotes a dean of a medical school in 1961: "Yes, indeed, we do take women, and we do not want that one woman to be lonesome, so we take two per class."[5] Nor did the modest expectations most women had about work before 1970 mean that secretaries and waitresses didn't enjoy the camaraderie at the workplace or the sense of purposefulness and accomplishment that come with a paycheck.

That said, most of the work available for women—and men, for that matter—was about as likely to evoke passion as an afternoon watching traffic go by. If given the choice, a lot of women, like the ur-disgruntled worker in "Bartleby the Scrivener," preferred not to. One Oklahoma woman described by Collins quit her job as a bookkeeper in the 1950s to raise her three children: "I guess I just like the freedom of being at home and not having someone tell me what to do."[6] Note the unexpected word "freedom": from this woman's vantage point, presumably shared by many like her, freedom is closer to housewifery than to a job at a canning factory or insurance office.

The success of feminism's siren call to the workplace, then, depended not just on removing discriminatory barriers but also on an economy that could provide a wealth of fulfilling jobs. That's exactly what the economy began to do. Middle-class women started scanning the help-wanted ads at precisely the moment when millions of jobs were opening up in the health sector, communications, public relations, consumer industries, and law. (Working-class women, it should go without saying, scanned the ads largely because their husbands' stagnating salaries were no longer enough to keep their families sheltered and fed.) Thinking about careers rather than jobs and fulfillment rather than a mere paycheck started to make sense. Had newly liberated women been staring at such jobs as truck driving or concrete mixing, it's an open question whether they would have thought that vacuuming was all that bad. (Betty Friedan, lest we forget, was a freelance writer.) *The Economist* nicely sums up the point: "The landmark book in the rise of feminism was arguably not Ms. Friedan's *The Feminine Mystique* but [sociologist] Daniel Bell's *The Coming of Post-Industrial Society.*"[7]

In fact, it's no exaggeration to say that the knowledge economy had as much to do with women's lives as the pill. Relying on physical strength and endurance, the industrial economy was a man's world. Perhaps there were women who could be men's equals working in the steel mills or on the auto line; digging in mines; building bridges; or laboring as lumberjacks, bricklayers, or roofers. But these were in the minority. Some people are inclined to wax romantic about these sorts of jobs. And it's true that in the heyday of the 1950s, industrial jobs provided the sort of security and comfort for workers that ordinary people could never have imagined in earlier centuries.

Those benefits can't erase the fact that those jobs were dirty, deafening, fume-filled, boring, physically strenuous, and often dangerous.[8] When the government started the iconic Rosie the Riveter propaganda campaign to get women into factories in order to replace men who had left for the World War II battlefields, officials knew they had a tough sales job. People didn't exactly *choose* a career on the factory floor. Cleveland *Plain Dealer* columnist Connie Schultz remembers her father, a maintenance man at the Cleveland Electric Illuminating Company, sometimes grumbling to himself, "You could teach a monkey to do what I do."[9] That's too harsh, maybe, but, Schultz writes, her father carried a lunch pail for thirty-six years in order to ensure that his children would never have to.

By the 1980s machines became more productive, communications and transportation cheaper and more efficient, and American manufacturing jobs began their storied decline. Increased productivity and competition on the manufacturing end meant less-expensive and better goods on the consumer end. Americans have been on a buying spree ever since, shopping not just for the kinds of things they found in stores and now on the Internet but also for such experiences as trips, yoga retreats, video games, and spas. Many things still had to be made, of course. But they also needed to be designed, planned, packaged, marketed, advertised, analyzed, shipped, and sold, as well as capitalized, regulated, and legalized.

Companies found that the making part could be done more cheaply elsewhere, and as everyone knows, a lot of factory work moved to Asia. What about the designing, planning, advertising, and so forth? Those activities stayed here and introduced millions of jobs in public relations, communications, marketing, and design as well as in finance and law. In addition, an increasingly competitive economy meant that people could no longer be counted on to buy GM or Colgate because that's what their parents did. That meant PR, marketing, and design became more central to industry, as essential as computer software is to hardware.[10] "There's so much 'noise' in the marketplace—so many competitors jockeying for position, so many products and services contending for space, so many messages and solicitations vying for attention—that customers may never find you," Robert Reich has written. "You occupy but one booth in a giant worldwide bazaar in which tens of millions of other sellers are trying to lure customers their way."[11]

Those jobs called on an entirely different range of human abilities from those that an economy based on processing steel or mining coal had, and it was a range in which women were easily men's equal. "Over the past decade, an era of rapid technological change and globalization, big employment gains came in occupations that rely on people skills and emotional intelligence," the Dallas Federal Reserve reported in 2003, though something similar could be said for the decade before:

> Over time, our work moves up a hierarchy of human talents, focusing on new tasks that require higher order skills. . . . Workers are increasingly using those traits that make us truly human. Some jobs require imagination and creativity, including the ability to design, innovate, and entertain. Other jobs rely on such social skills as conflict resolution, cooperation and even humor. Work is more likely to put a premium on the ability to inspire and motivate, a capacity social scientists call emotional intelligence.[12]

Between 1992 and 2002, the report continues, of the "jobs that involve imagination and creativity," designers increased their ranks by 44 percent, actors and directors by 61 percent, and architects by 44 percent. Jobs using "analytic reasoning" also increased; lawyers went up by 24 percent between 1970 and 1983, a time that also saw a large jump in the number of doctors.[13] Some of these jobs have undoubtedly been lost in the Great Recession, but the basic point still holds: over the past decades, knowledge jobs exploded in both number and breadth, a windfall for young women now planning for stimulating careers, as well as for the employers who benefited from their drive and talents.

It may not be pleasant to say so, then, but manufacturing's loss has been women's gain. To this day, those holding jobs in manufacturing are more than 70 percent male; construction is about 88 percent guys, much as it has always been. In 2008, women accounted for 51 percent of all workers in management and professional occupations, more than their share of total employment.[14] According to the Department of Labor, 46 and 41 percent of employed Asian and white women worked in these high-paying areas. Women outnumbered men in such occupations as public relations managers, financial managers, human resource managers, education administrators, medical and health services managers, accountants and auditors, budget analysts, and writers and authors.[15] The education and health services sector is also 77 percent female.

To better grasp the transformation from the industrial to the knowledge economy that has especially benefited young women, let's examine one profession mentioned in the Dallas Fed report: design.[16] We could only talk about design as a profession relatively recently. True, since they first left their caves, human beings have designed their everyday objects: clothes, huts, and cooking and eating implements. In this sense, design has always been with us. In preindustrial times, furniture makers, tailors and seamstresses, cobblers, and metalworkers were de facto designers. But it was only at the turn of the twentieth century, not coincidentally just as machines were taking over the production of everyday objects, that design became a profession and the designer a self-conscious actor in the marketplace. The artists of the famous Bauhaus school launched the field of industrial—sometimes called "product"—design when they saw the aesthetic possibilities of everyday manufactured objects, such as radios and teakettles. Several decades earlier, color lithography gave birth to graphic design as merchants grasped the potential for posters to bring attention to their products; ironically, their *Normandie* vessel and Moulin Rouge nightclub posters had more staying power than the goods they advertised. There was fashion design, of course, but it was a small and rarefied profession with a customer base limited to a very particular elite.

For most of the twentieth century in the United States, outside of a few big names such as Charles and Ray Eames, the design profession occupied an ill-defined status somewhere between electrician and ad executive. Parents dreaming of the good life for their children might imagine their becoming lawyers or doctors. But designers? Designers got their hands dirty, like plumbers or auto mechanics, and their jobs were reminiscent of the working-class life many old-timers were trying to escape. Art directors in ad agencies were so low in the corporate hierarchy that copywriters sometimes referred to them as "wrists." "Winston tastes good like a cigarette should" was the key to product success, not banal pictures of a cigarette box.

It was modern technology, specifically the digital revolution, and economic growth that gave us the multivaried contemporary design profession. Computers separated rote and technical work—typesetting, drafting, drawing—from higher-order cognitive skills, propelling designers from the ranks of ink-stained wretches to that of postindustrial knowledge worker. Computers made it possible for designers to work faster and more innovatively. In the era before computers, "when you had to order typeset, you couldn't experiment," says Eric Baker of Eric Baker Design. "It was much too expensive. And it took overnight." Today, in that same amount of time, "you can do thirty versions."[17] Constantly improving and more affordable computer-aided design (CAD) software—Photoshop is the best-known of many—was also coming on the market. Three-dimensional computer-aided design—generally known as "3D CAD"—allows industrial designers to create prototypes of such simple products as sunglasses or toothbrushes that go straight to the manufacturer. CAD also makes it easier to customize products, as the designers using Solidworks software did in the well-publicized case of Malia and Sasha Obama's swingset standing on the White House lawn.

Luckily for the design-conscious preadult, the digital revolution expanded the very meaning of design. On the most obvious level, computers introduced the field of web design. Ten years ago, a company might hire a graphic designer—or maybe just a skilled relative—to create a brochure and business cards. Today people want websites: fancy websites—with animation, audio and video insets, clever drawings or photos, links, and user-friendly navigation tools—that, unlike brochures, could change with the season or zeitgeist and that only highly trained professionals could create. "The Internet entailed not only the explosion of information but also the *aestheticization of information*," writes Vanderbilt sociologist Richard Lloyd in *Neo-Bohemia: Art and Commerce in the Post-industrial City*.[18] Young tech-savvy designers have found new careers in infographics (turning data and information into visual form) video animation, and game and user interface design (the job of making everyday web users at ease with technology by creating easy-to-use links and drop-down tabs).

In fact, for the postdigital design generation, it is becoming increasingly difficult to fix a clear boundary line between technology and design. More efficient computer chips and improvements in circuitry and plastics often do more to determine the aesthetics of an object than color and decorative detail. Design, in Apple founder Steve Jobs's well-known formulation, is "how it works." Apple's MP3 player, the beloved iPod, designed by a team headed by the British designer Jonathan Ive, embodies the contemporary marriage of design and technology. Like the artists of the Bauhaus school, Steve Jobs wanted his company to "stand at the intersection between technology and the arts."[19] And so it did. Today, every appliance maker is in a race to do for the toaster or radio what Apple did for the computer and MP3 player.

Globalization also helped propel design into the realm of a high-status profession. When Photoshop first appeared, graphic artists in particular worried that the technological revolution energizing their business would be its undoing. After all, desktop publishing democratized design, making it possible for any 12-year-old to distinguish between Times New Roman and Verdana typefaces. Paradoxically, as Virginia Postrel points out in her important 2003 book *The Substance of Style,* the opposite happened. Cheap labor markets in China, Thailand, and India allowed an explosion of designed objects that educated the public eye, which in turn raised the bar for more attractive shoes, children's clothes, handbags, and furniture. More and more people wanted to pick up their furniture from Target or Pottery Barn, not Sears or Montgomery Ward. Globalization has made clothing cheaper than at any time in history; it now only takes up less than 4 percent of household spending, even as silk, linen, and cashmere have become ubiquitous.[20] Suburban mall rats have learned to discriminate colors, styles, fabrics, and fonts the way their ancestors could spot the differences among genera of tall grass. Before, Postrel observes, "aesthetics was a specialized good available mostly in a few large urban markets." By the last decade of the twentieth century, we had entered a mass "age of aesthetics."[21]

In the age of aesthetics, no business can afford to be indifferent to design. How do you distinguish your camera or washing machine from the crowds of other cameras and washing machines that perform more or less as well and at approximately the same price? Of course: good design. Design has become so key to product success that designers have been summoned from their remote studio offices to work directly with corporate strategists and marketers to plan future products and to coordinate advertising campaigns. Corporate recruiters woo design school students; business schools do case studies of design as corporate strategy. "The MFA is the new MBA," the writer Daniel Pink has announced, an obvious exaggeration but a suggestive one.[22]

And there's more. Let's say someone has a business selling, I don't know, cardboard boxes and wants to expand his market. He might decide to hire a "design anthropologist," a scholar who studies people using products in their native habitat—in other words, their home or office—to figure out how to improve the cardboard box user's experience. (Microsoft has sent anthropologists to developing countries to help the company understand how different cultures use technology.) He might look into employing a design psychologist who can advise him about how the brain reacts to the color and shape of those cardboard boxes. Don't forget the "experiential designer," who can advise him on the emotions and sensory engagement of potential cardboard box customers. ESI, a New York–based experiential design firm, for instance, revamped some of the Best Buy warehouse-like mega-stores into interactive village-like spaces with six "experience-based zones" where buyers are encouraged to test out games or watch plasma TVs in comfy chairs. If the cardboard box seller is so inclined, he can pay a "strategic designer" to help him do some long-range planning.

So what does this have to do with the New Girl Order? In the not-so-distant past, the design business was pretty much a man's world. In the 1960s, says Eric Baker, graphic design was a closed fraternity; there were few women in art departments or design studios, just as there were few in law offices or medical schools.[23] Of course, there were always über-talented women who made it in the business, including such legendary figures as Coco Chanel and Sister Parrish. But they tended to work primarily in women's fashion and interior decorating, and given the expense of clothes and home decor in the era before globalization, the number of potential customers was very small. These days, men continue to dominate the tech side of design. When there is code to be written, as there is in web design, there tends to be a guy doing it,[24] though that might be changing. There is a crowd of websites for girl techies: Geekfeminism.org; Girlsintech.com; or Geekgirlcamp .com, a group that launched a successful Internet campaign to name "computer engineer" the next career for the Barbie doll in a Mattel contest.[25]

In other parts of the design world, however, women are more than making up for lost time. In fact, design is a major industry of the New Girl Order. Women now make up 60 percent of design school students, and design studios are full of 'em. They are increasingly prominent in graphic and product design. Deborah Adler is a fine example.

The daughter of a New York doctor and nurse, Adler graduated from the University of Vermont before she went on for her master's degree at the School of Visual Arts. At about the time she was searching for a thesis topic, her grandmother accidentally swallowed prescription pills meant for her grandfather. Looking in their medicine cabinet later, Adler realized why: prescription bottles were confusing, which to shrewd design types like Adler meant they were poorly designed. And so for her thesis, Adler created a new label with the name of the drug instead of the pharmacy in bold at the top, colored rings at the neck of the bottle indicating the person in the household using the drug, a flat instead of a curved surface to be more readable, and more user-friendly warning signals. Target was taken with the creation she called "Safe RX." The company revamped its computer software and pharmacy procedures around the new container and label, while Adler went on to work at the studio of the legendary Milton Glaser, where she designed other medical products for safety and efficiency.[26]

Adler's utilitarian example aside, it's probably in retail design—clothing, accessories, and household objects—that women are making their biggest mark. This makes sense; as the management maven Tom Peters has noted, "Women buy most stuff, hence women should design most stuff."[27] Women have always been families' consumers-in-chief, and despite the changes in domestic life, they still are. They're the ones deciding about clothes, furniture, rugs, vases, plates, linens, pots, and pans, as well as detergent and toilet paper. As women went to work, their consumer needs—and the opportunities for designers—only increased. Not only did they have to purchase business clothing (the pantsuit was introduced by Yves St. Laurent in 1966 at first as evening wear in imitation of a tuxedo, but soon after as much-needed office attire), they also had to find services and products to renovate domestic and office life to suit their new roles—takeout meals, cell phones, microwavable food, totes for holding books and laptops, and planners. The futurist Faith Popcorn adds another, less predictable product inspired by the working woman: stress reducers. Here's her formula: "(x) more stress plus (y) more cash equals (z) more ways to relax," including aromatherapy candles and diffusers, lotions, spas, and Jacuzzis. (By the late 1990s, scented candles—my guess is that you don't know any men who buy them—were more than a billion-dollar-a-year business, sold in boutiques, department stores, pharmacies, and cosmetics emporiums.)[28]

Women are not only still in charge of domestic purchases. Their contribution to household income—and in a growing number of cases, their role as primary breadwinner—gives them more influence over such large purchases as cars, homes, appliances, insurance policies, and family vacations. According to Popcorn, they buy 50 percent of all PCs and cars; they are 48 percent of stock market investors. "Women now drive the world economy," say Michael Silverstein and Kate Sayre in the *Harvard Business Review*. "Globally, they control about $20 trillion in annual consumer spending, and that figure could climb as high as $28 trillion in the next five years. Their $13 trillion in total yearly earnings could reach $18 trillion in the same period. In aggregate, women represent a growth market bigger than China and India combined—more than twice as big."[29]

Young women—preadults—may still be earning starting salaries, but they are no slouches when it comes to buying stuff. Their economic impact is great enough that *The Economist* invented the term "Bridget Jones Economy."[30] By the 1990s, says a principal of London-based Intelligence Factory in its 2004 report "The Single Female Consumer," "women living alone had come to comprise the strongest consumer block in much the same way that yuppies did in the 1980s."[31] Single Young Females—SYFs in marketese—are the engine behind the growth of apparel stores devoted to stylish career wear, such as Ann Taylor, which now has more than 800 stores in the United States; the international Zara, with more than 1,000 stores in 54 countries; H&M; and more recently, the British Topshop. Enthusiasm for shopping peaks when a woman is in her twenties and when she's 55 and older, says Frank About Women marketing director Carrie McCament, mostly because any extra money they have, they can spend on themselves. Shopping is something like a sport for young women ("Shopping is my cardio," goes Carrie's T-shirt-worthy quip from *Sex and the City*), part competition ("They want to be the best-dressed person in their groups," says McCament) and part socializing.[32]

The Bridget Jones Economy also includes things that don't need to be buttoned or zipped: nail salons, spas, yoga and Pilates studios, sweetish coffee concoctions and cocktails, and the trendy cafés and bars where these drinks are served. I won't say these things didn't exist twenty-five years ago, but they were exceedingly rare. Electronics manufacturers design products especially for young women; take a gander at Nintendo DS Lite, described as "cute and small and portable"—and now available in pink. Car, video game, packaging, and liquor manufacturers are on the make for female buyers. Young women also spend their paychecks at Sephora, the Paris-based cosmetics emporium that targets younger women in fourteen countries. Sephora opened its first store in the United States in 1997; today, there are 126 all over North America. In 2003 the Diamond Trading Company introduced the "right-hand ring," a diamond for women with no marital prospects but longing for a rock. "Your left hand is your heart; your right hand is your voice," one ad promises.

The point here is not that preadult women are vain, material girls. On the contrary, women are more likely than men to work in the nonprofit arena and to volunteer their time in homeless shelters and soup kitchens. And let's not forget that designers are often making their own contribution to the public good, either by creating useful products—remember Deborah Adler—or by starting new businesses that create jobs for other workers.

Still, the uncomfortable truth is that youthful female careerism is closely intertwined with the growth of consumption for two reasons. First, working women make and spend a lot of money. Second, women can find satisfying (passion-filled?) careers centered around the sorts of products on which women like to spend money. Most new businesses started by American women are retail or service oriented. Many of them are design related. As technology advances, women are in an even better position to improve their standing. Gregory Ericksen, author of *Women Entrepreneurs Only*, puts it this way: "In the 'one-on-one economy,' you have to understand the unique needs of the customer you're working with to be successful. Mass manufacturing, mass marketing doesn't play out any more. Even mass customization doesn't play out any more. But customization on demand does. And that takes an entrepreneur who can sense what the customer wants and how that's different from other customers." And those entrepreneurs, says Ericksen, are women.[33]

Chloe Dao, one of seven daughters of Laotian immigrants growing up in Houston, is a fairy tale example of the New Girl Order designer/entrepreneur. Like many immigrants, her parents dreamt of medical and law degrees for their children; unfortunately, or at least it seemed that way at the time, Chloe seemed mostly interested in clothes. She was ambitious enough to design and sew her own prom dress, but her future must have seemed inauspicious, especially after she dropped out of college her first semester. Eventually, though, she made her way to the Fashion Institute of Design in New York, and after going through a variety of fashion and marketing jobs, opened her own boutique in Houston. In 2006, she won on the second season of *Project Runway*, the popular Bravo reality show, and was quickly signed by Designers Management Agency, a company that does for designers what Creative Artists Agency does for actors and directors. She now has her own clothing line, as well as a contract with Pacific Design to create cases for iPods and other electronic devices for sale at Office Depot and Target.[34] What would Dao have been doing a generation ago? In all likelihood, her design career would have ended with her prom dress and maybe birthday presents for her kids. In the girl-powered design economy, she's a player.

Dao has hit the big time, but there are plenty of young female design entrepreneurs following their bliss by starting small cottage businesses. Ironic as it seems, a high-tech knowledge economy has paved the way for a revival of artisan-style production that is more reminiscent of a "craftsman" era than an industrial time. It doesn't take all that much capital or risk to customize production with a computer, just as it doesn't take a large staff to network and promote a business once you have the Internet. Some young designers never do a business plan or spreadsheet; they stumble into a jewelry or stationery business after making a necklace or card for family, friends, then friends of friends, and so forth. It helps that they often live in neo-bohemia, as Richard Lloyd dubs the once-gritty neighborhoods of Los Angeles, Brooklyn, and Chicago where young metalsmiths, letterpress printers, and lighting and graphic designers are cross-pollinating ideas and business contacts in retro-fitted factories. If they're really lucky like Dao, they might be tapped by talent scouts for larger retail outlets.

Sarah Cihat and Jill Malek, both Brooklyn design entrepreneurs, illustrate the revival. Like other young designers, as a young adult Cihat was at a loss for what to do with her life. She dropped out after a semester at the University of Tennessee; "I knew there was nothing there for me," she now says. Fortunately, she found her way to Parsons School of Design, where her thesis project—reglazing and painting thrift shop dishes in bright colors with bold graphics—has led to a thriving business. Today, the 30-year-old Brooklyn artist sells both her old/new dishes and candles in partnership with the Joya candle company to a growing number of "green" consumers at such places as Barneys and LouisBoston.

Her fellow Brooklynite Jill Malek was a fine arts major at Oberlin with little interest in commercial design. After graduating from college and in need of a job, she learned graphic design and took a number of corporate jobs. During that time, she developed her "skill set" and, realizing that "the fine artist in me was not fulfilled," she started her own business. At 32, she designs websites, stationery, and invitations as well as hand-screened wallpaper from her apartment in Brooklyn Heights. As in the case of Cihat and Dao, the design economy has allowed her to spread her aesthetic vision into entirely unforeseen areas; she recently signed a deal with Yogamatic to create a line of yoga mats.

Design is far from the only industry that rode the tsunami of the knowledge economy with jobs that would be especially appealing to women. Over the past decades, the economy has also multiplied the career possibilities in the arena broadly described as "communications."

Not that there's anything new about women in communication-rich jobs. From early on in American life, women were tapped as schoolteachers, librarians, and salesgirls. In the late nineteenth century, the just-established telephone companies hired teenage boys to be operators. Because they had staffed telegraph offices, it seemed a sensible arrangement. As it happened, though, the boys were lousy operators: impatient, impolite, and with an irritating tendency to play pranks on customers. Women were called in to rescue the fledgling industry. The phone companies got a twofer: they found polite, mature workers who also worked on the cheap because at the time, women were not paid much more than adolescent boys.[35]

Women also found an early if uneasy foothold in the publishing industry, first as authors and journalists, and over time as editors and publishers. Women have made up more than half of the nation's reading audience of both magazines and books for a long time, so it's not so surprising that they would also take to the pen. In the nineteenth century, the author Nathaniel Hawthorne complained about the "damned mobs of scribbling women."[36] Those scribblers mostly produced novels and advice books about domestic or family matters, but there were some—such as Harriet Beecher

Stowe, the renowned author of *Uncle Tom's Cabin,* and her friend Helen Hunt Jackson, whose 1884 novel *Ramona* explored the poor treatment of Indians—with weightier topics in mind. By 1919, there were enough women in the news business to justify a Women's National Press Club, and a few of them—muckraking journalists Nellie Bly and Ida Tarbell come to mind—had real influence on both public discussion and their profession. Still, the most prominent female names in journalism through most of the first half of the twentieth century were editors at *Ladies' Home Journal* and *McCall's*—in other words, those who were confined to the ladies' magazine ghetto. Until the 1970s, the few aspiring women at such general news outlets as *Newsweek* were generally delegated to lower-status research and fact-checking jobs.[37]

But the scribblers quickly expanded both sideways and upward in the publishing world. In fact, their success in the publishing industry was intricately connected to their growing political and economic power. It's striking how many of the most prominent second-wave feminists were ink-stained. Betty Friedan did the original research that culminated in *The Feminine Mystique* for *Ladies' Home Journal;* Gloria Steinem wrote for *Esquire* and *New York* magazine; Robin Morgan was a poet and writer. In the 1970s, the women's movement flooded the nonfiction zone with memoirs and manifestos; it helped that they found an expanding sisterhood in literary agencies and publishing houses.[38] Women were close to 50 percent of all book editors in 1970.[39] By 1973, they were 47 percent of new reporter and editor hires at the *New York Times,* compared to 7 percent in the years before.[40]

This was only the early days of the publishing-rich knowledge economy. If they are inclined toward a career in print, today's preadult women will find an industry not only friendly to them but filled with possibilities that did not exist in their mothers' day.

At the moment—I'm writing in April 2010, when every week seems to shutter another paper or magazine—this may appear almost perversely wrong. A devastating recession and seismic changes in media and advertising delivery seem to have all but decimated the newspaper and magazine business. More than 100 newspapers have closed their doors, 10,000 jobs have been lost, and even the largest-circulation papers are hemorrhaging readers.[41] Yes, it's bad right now. The longer view, looking back and toward the future, though, tells a different story. In 1973, there were 3,000 book publishers, according to *Publishers Weekly*; by 2004, despite the arrival of rapacious international conglomerates, there were about 85,000.[42]

Today, women constitute more than 65 percent of bachelor's, 68 percent of master's, and about 58 percent of doctoral degrees in journalism.[43] Journalism school applications are way up.[44] Are these aspiring scribblers crazy? Not at all. Although the decade between 1997 and 2006 saw a small decrease in the percentage of the population reading magazines, the population grew enough that there was an overall increase in readership. And print is still where the girls are. The fastest growth in readership has been of the female persuasion; there remain forty-one magazines targeting women, as opposed to only twenty-five for men.[45] This is true despite increasing competition for attention from cable and network television and the Internet. According to the Bureau of Labor Statistics, by 2016, the number of positions for entry-level reporters and news anchors will increase 2 percent, while those for experienced writers and editors will grow 10 percent.[46]

The young female striver might also consider a job on television without someone looking at her like she should stop being a little girl playing with her Television Anchor Barbie. Over the past decades, improvements in technology have given us more specialization, more demand, and a rapid growth in such cable networks as Oxygen, HGTV, and Golf TV. Jobs grew, and so did the female presence. By the 1990s, there were as many women as men at the anchor desk; as of 2006, they held 57 percent of news anchor jobs. They also made up 58 percent of reporters, 56 percent of news writers, 66 percent of producers, and 55 percent of executive producers. Journalism professors and broadcast executives both observe a bailout by the onetime "first sex": "There's been an evacuation of men from this field," notes one academic. At the highest levels in the executive offices, men may continue to be in the majority, but given the women coming through the pipeline, it won't be that way for long.[47] Meanwhile, the government predicts 7.4 percent growth in broadcasting jobs over the next ten years, lower than a lot of industries, but not a number that should demoralize aspiring anchors.[48]

And let's not forget the Internet as an outlet for female communicators; iVillage, one of the biggest Internet success stories, has plenty of competition from Network for Women, MSN Women, Oprah.com, and many others. *Business Insider* looked at the top twenty-five journalists successfully making the move from old to new media. More than half of them were women, including Tina Brown; Arianna Huffington; Jill Lawrence, who moved from *USA Today* to *Politics Daily*; and Cheryl Brown, onetime editor of *Gourmet* and now at AOL's KitchenDaily.com.[49]

Jobs in marketing and public relations are another example of the female-dominated communications explosion. The Bureau of Labor Statistics has listed public relations as one of the three fastest-growing industries in the United States, right behind computer and data processing and health services. According to Glen Broom, a professor at the School of Communications at San Diego State University, the industry has doubled in size in the last fifteen years; now, he says, there are close to 350,000 public relations professionals in the United States. Starting in the 1980s, there was a huge influx of women into the field. Today, with 70 percent of PR jobs going to women, the career is almost entirely an all-girls club.[50] Judging from the demographics of public relations classrooms in college, the business may become even more of a female domain in the near future.[51] There are no official data, but event planning, a small and relatively new profession and one predicted to have a healthy future, appears to be largely female.[52] The hospitality industry has also seen a surge in the number of women—and at the highest levels.[53]

If their presence in popular culture is proof of anything, communications jobs are very enticing to young women. One of the first sitcom career girls was Mary Richards of *The Mary Tyler Moore Show*, who was an associate producer for a six o'clock news show at a Minneapolis television station. Mary was no Darren Star creation; as a 30-year-old single woman in the 1970s, she had a hint of melancholy about her ("You're going to make it after all!" went the determinedly upbeat lyrics). But she was followed in the 1980s by the aggressively glamorous Murphy Brown, whose job as an anchor and investigative reporter reflected the growing prestige of women in the workplace, and whose personal life illustrated their freedom in the reproductive realm. (Murphy Brown, as anyone older than 12 at the time can attest, became a single mother and a major culture-war flashpoint.)

Communications, especially writing, is also the career choice of an impressive number of heroines of the popular chick lit genre, the romance novel for the young urban knowledge worker. The mega–chick lit hit *Bridget Jones's Diary* (public relations assistant) spawned a brood of chick novels set in London, including Sophie Kinsella's *Confessions of a Shopaholic* (magazine writer) and Jane Green's best-selling *Mr. Maybe* (public relations assistant). The heroine of the best-selling *Good in Bed* is the pop culture reporter for the fictional Philadelphia *Examiner*. *Run, Catch, Kiss* (sex columnist); *Slightly Single* (assistant book editor); and *Confessions of an Ex-Girlfriend* (writer for a bridal magazine) all follow the same lines. In best-selling *The Devil Wears Prada*, the heroine leaves her job as an editor's assistant with the dream of becoming a writer at the *New Yorker*. By the end of the novel, she is selling her articles to *Seventeen*, which in the chick-lit universe apparently means you'll soon be attending Christmas parties with Malcolm Gladwell. The novel, by the way, became a movie that the citizens of the New Girl Order turned into an international sensation.

The queen of chick-lit heroines, sex and relationship columnist Carrie Bradshaw, provides the ultimate proof that "writer" represents the fairy tale career for young romantics, as prized as Mr. Big himself. On one episode of *Sex and the City*, Carrie is asked to model clothes for a charity benefit and objects with the astute self-mockery typical of the show at its best: "I can't strut out in jeweled panties in front of Frank Rich. I respect Frank Rich. Frank Rich is a *writer*." The knowledge economy worker prides herself on being more expressive, more real than the 1950s Organization Man whose job demanded order, formality, and inauthenticity. But deep down, she has her doubts; even in the creative economy, work cannot welcome every part of identity. Writing—creative, expressive, simultaneously public and private—seems to promise greater wholeness, allowing the worker to scout depths that most jobs, even in the knowledge economy, ask us to leave in our journals. Or so it seems.

Design, fiction writing, journalism, public relations, marketing, event planning, managing: these are jobs for people who can communicate, persuade, charm, and multitask, who score high on empathy, intuition, communication skills, planning, and relationship building. Hmm. These sound familiar. In fact, they sound suspiciously like those old stereotypes about women, the ones that were used to explain why they were meant to be the "angel in the house."

Does this career sorting imply that women *are* from Venus, naturally more adept at interpersonal communication and empathy than men? Does that explain why they become PR managers and fashion designers?[54] And does all of this suggest, in turn, that men *are* from Mars, more inclined to abstract and systematic thinking, which is why they dominate in the sciences and engineering?[55] We know at this point that there are differences between the sexes in brain structure, chemistry, neuron density, the number of synapses, and circuitry. What remains unclear is precisely how these differences translate into behavior, or if they do at all. For instance, girls and women of all ages are better at defining emotions on faces than boys and men.[56] But the differences are small at young ages and intensify as people get older. That could mean that women's putative empathy advantage is largely because of doll manufacturers and the parents who support them.[57] On the other hand, it could mean that the female infant's greater capacity for interpersonal awareness grows more quickly once all brain cylinders are firing. So which is it? Nature, nurture, or some combination of both?

For our purposes, thankfully, *it doesn't matter*. Even if men and women had precisely the same natural ability to, say, write computer code on the one hand or press releases on the other, it would be impossible to alter the culture in a generation, or two, or possibly even three in ways that would lead to a state of pure androgyny in the labor market. The fact for young people coming of age today and for the foreseeable future is that women are more drawn to, and are often better at, many of the organizational skills prized in the knowledge economy. In a 2002 paper called "Where the Boys Aren't," Harvard economist Brian Jacob compared a large cohort of college grads who had been eighth-graders in 1988. He found that whereas boys and girls scored similarly on cognitive tests, girls were stronger at "noncognitive" tasks—paying attention in class, organizing, keeping track of homework, and collaborating with classmates. Jacobs posits that girls' strengths in these areas explain the college gender gap. It's reasonable to conclude that 22-year-olds probably bring the same organizational and communicative strengths or weaknesses to the workplace.[58] Another 2006 paper shows how between the late 1970s and the 1990s, "people skills" became more crucial for success in the labor market. Not coincidentally, say the authors, this was the period when women's wages rose rapidly.[59]

By all accounts, women are better at remembering those hand-written thank-you notes after interviews and lunches as well as clients' and contacts' birthdays. They also excel at networking and mentoring. It's easy to get lost in the thicket of Internet meeting places where women network, share ideas, and find inspiration, including—in addition to the already-mentioned iVillage, Oxygen, and Oprah.com—Wiredwoman and Womanconnect.com.[60] (Out of curiosity, I checked out Manconnect.com. It turns out to be "where REAL men connect with men of the REAL world" through a gallery of beefcake photos. Is this what men mean by networking?) The consulting company Copernicus found similar views about women's people skills in a survey of senior marketing executives. The company did two surveys, one in 1998 and the other in 2008. Men were perceived by both men and women as more aggressive and insensitive and women as more consensus-building and caring in both surveys. In fact, the gender differences had increased during the course of the decade.[61] One of the reasons women find computer careers uninviting is that the work tends to be lonely, especially when it goes on, as it often does, for 60 hours a week. Says one female engineer about why she left her first job to start her own company: "The guys went into their rooms and coded all day."[62] She wanted to be interacting with human beings, not machines.

So if women are so great, why aren't they running the place? Many experts believe that time is coming, not so much because in the future everyone will be gender-blind, but because the knowledge economy workplace requires a more feminine style of leadership. Modern management theorists look down on the hierarchical arrangements and competitive individualism of yesterday's office. Instead they advise executives to promote a sense of community and teamwork. For followers of the Mars/Venus paradigm, this is clearly good news for women. "Men have tended to do better in the hierarchies, following orders and relying on positional power," one Washington, DC, consultant told *Business-Week*.[63] Women, on the other hand, support and engage workers.[64] The business literature is crowded with articles and books sporting such titles as "How to Get a Great Executive? Hire a Female," "The Future of Business Depends on Women," and *Why the Best Man for the Job Is a Woman*.[65]

This leads to a more subtle and vexing implication of the Mars/Venus career divide. A substantial amount of research points to the conclusion that women and men don't simply prefer different careers. They actually think differently about what role work should play in their lives. Women tend to choose careers more on the basis of what psychologists call "intrinsic rewards." That is, they are less likely to put money, power, and status at the center of their ambitions, and are more inclined to think about other sorts of satisfaction.[66] A 2004 study entitled "Off-Ramps and On-Ramps: Keeping Talented Women on the Road to Success" found that six other goals—colleagues, "bringing myself" to work, flexibility, collaboration and teamwork, recognition, and giving back to society—trump money and power for women.[67] "Research has shown that women tend to gravitate toward fields of studies and career paths where they can have a positive social impact and work with others, often collaboratively. This is why you see so many women in the fields of health care and education. When women do gravitate toward the sciences, it is usually the life sciences."[68] Sound like something Reverend Evangelical might say? Actually, that was Linda Basch, president of the National Council for Research on Women (NCRW), an organization promoting women's workplace equity, among other things.

Admittedly, some of the research about intrinsic and extrinsic rewards is dated, and the findings are not robust enough to make stark generalizations about the differences in men's and women's preferences. Let's be clear: men also want intrinsic satisfactions in their work, even if they don't rank them as highly as women do. Likewise, women want to make money. However, the conclusions of the values research are entirely in keeping with a number of facts. Women are disproportionately represented in lower-paying nonprofit jobs. Three out of four fund-raisers are female,[69] and 55 percent of all chief executive or chief grant-making jobs are held by women (though the CEOs of the major charities are usually male).[70] Women with law degrees are considerably more likely to practice public interest law than men.[71] The government sector is 57 percent female.[72] One more related fact: women undergrads make up 78 percent of psychology majors and 61 percent of humanities majors.[73] They are 60 percent of the doctorates in social and behavioral sciences, 70 percent in health sciences, but only 38 percent in business and 33 percent in physical and earth sciences.[74] These are not the choices of future Mistresses of the Universe.

In other words, women disproportionately choose lower-paying careers. Nonprofit salaries are measly compared to the private sector, and a degree in history is unlikely to lead to the big bucks that a degree in computing or finance might. Economists Claudia Goldin and Mark Katz looked at the careers of Harvard MBAs who graduated between 1990 and 2006. Right after entering the job market, men and women had almost identical incomes. Ten years later, men were way ahead. They found one primary reason: women with children took time away from their jobs and worked shorter hours than men.[75] However, they also noted that MBA women with no children were still earning 12 percent less than equivalent men. Why? "Mainly because they were employed by smaller firms, and disproportionately in the nonprofit sector."[76]

The question then is why. Do they care less about how much money they make? In surveys, women rank financial self-sufficiency high on their list of goals. Are women less materialistic than men? Somehow, that seems unlikely. Still, the truth is, as they ponder their career choices, women—and that includes the millennial women of the New Girl Order—can realistically imagine a broader range of scenarios for their lives than their brothers can. We know from surveys that the large majority of women expect to marry and have children someday. Under those circumstances, they might imagine scenario number 1: working part-time or even taking time off to have more time with their kids. That's a pretty common approach; about a third of highly qualified women leave the workforce voluntarily for an average of 2.7 years. Of these, 73 percent later go back to work, but only 40 percent of those find full-time jobs.[77] Scenario number 2: patching together something like a full-time job by sharing childcare with their husbands, also a common story. Scenario number 3: hiring a nanny or relying on relatives so they can continue their careers with minimal interruption.

The scenario they probably *don't* imagine is this: supporting a stay-at-home husband and children. Yes, it's true that an increasing number of women are earning more than their husbands; given the successes of women, those numbers could grow. And there are more Mr. Moms doing the diaper changing, school pickups, and such, though the numbers remain extremely small.[78] But is that a scenario most women want? Ask working fathers if they would prefer part-time jobs, and 21 percent say yes. Ask working mothers, and it's 62 percent; that's a 14-point increase from ten years ago, by the way.[79] Even in female-friendly Scandinavia, women take far more family leave than men, despite governments' persistent efforts to have men go 50/50.[80] No doubt, adding to women's part-time preference are the demands of the contemporary workplace. I have argued that the knowledge economy has been good for women, and in most respects it has. But that economy tends to produce a lot of fast-paced, emotionally and cognitively challenging work. The knowledge economy "is predicated on change and speed," Richard Florida writes. "The employees must be constantly finding faster, cheaper, or better ways to do things. . . . It's brutally stressful."[81] And for many mothers who try it, even more so.

What all of this suggests is that young women can approach work in a less utilitarian and more self-expressive frame of mind than young men. Men know that if marriage and family are in the cards, the pressure is on to work and earn. They may not choose a career solely for its money quotient, but the subject tends to loom large in their minds. Women want to know they can be self-sufficient, and if they have a family, to bring in enough to be a competent financial partner to their husbands. Where money is concerned, there's a motivation gap. As they set out to design their futures, women can afford to take a more romantic view of work, to think in terms of passion and self-development. As the economist Claudia Goldin has written about the "quiet revolution" that took place after 1970 when women began to move into the labor force in big numbers: "It was a change from agents who work because they and their families 'need the money' to those who are employed, at least in part, because occupation and employment define one's fundamental identity and societal worth. It involved a change from 'jobs' to 'careers.'"[82] This may understate how important a second salary is to couples, even those with a lot of degrees after their names. But it captures a subtle dynamic behind the gender gap.

How did that Monster.com motto put it? "Work. Life. Possibilities"? Well, for women, maybe.

four

CHILD-MAN IN
THE PROMISED LAND

Here's a cultural mystery for you: Adam Sandler. The list of Sandler hit movies began in 1995 with *Billy Madison*, the story of a porn-watching 28-year-old who goes back to elementary school. Then there was *Happy Gilmore*, about a loser (janitor, security guard, gas station attendant, etc.) who dreams of becoming a professional hockey player despite the fact that he can't skate. After hitting several people with golf balls from a distance, he discovers a talent for the sport and proceeds to bring his puerile tantrums to the PGA tour. In *The Wedding Singer*, a wannabe rock star has a backup career, and in *Big Daddy*, a law school–grad slacker living off insurance from a car accident hangs out with an orphaned boy to impress his girlfriend, and they do little boy things together. Jokes about pee, vomit, spit, feces, farting, Hooters, breasts, and sex, and people falling out of windows, being eaten by crocodiles, and getting hit by golf balls are what pass for plot. In the animated *Eight Crazy Nights*, Sandler does the voice-over for Davey Stone, a 32-year-old loner. "If you like fart jokes, rude songs about body parts and buckets full of poop, then this is the movie for you," assures one Internet site. At 43, Sandler's most recent cinematic effort at the time of this writing is *Grown Ups* (it's a joke, get it?), about a group of aging ex–basketball buddies. "I'm not particularly talented. I'm not particularly good-looking. And yet I'm a multi-millionaire," Sandler told an audience during his press tour for the movie.[1]

Yes, but as he well knows, Sandler is one of the inventors and *the* yogic master of the new genre of male arrested development. *That* is what makes him a multimillionaire. The actor has shown another, more thoughtful side in several films (e.g., *Spanglish*, *Funny People*), but they garnered only anemic response from audiences. It's the arrested-development films that have made him one of the biggest stars in Hollywood, with movies totaling $2.5 billion worldwide. Which leads us to the question: What are these films, anyway? They're not screwball comedy; they're not vaudeville, physical slapstick, or romantic comedy; God knows they're not Oscar Wilde. No, they're comedy for child-men, a genre of our times.

Not so coincidentally, the same decade that brought us the girl-powered preadult and built the foundations for the New Girl Order introduced a contradictory cultural type and the source of Sandler's fortune: the child-man. The child-man is the fun house mirror image of the alpha girl. If she is ambitious, he is a slacker. If she is hyper-organized and self-directed, he tends toward passivity and vagueness. If she is preternaturally mature, he is happily not. Their opposition is stylistic as well: she drinks sophisticated cocktails in mirrored bars, he burps up beer on ratty sofas. She spends her hard-earned money on mani-pedi outings, his goes toward *World of Warcraft* and gadgets. If her aspirational hero is the urbane Carrie Bradshaw (or was until the disaster that is the movie *Sex and the City 2*), his is, well, the potty-mouthed and -brained Adam Sandler.

Twenty or thirty years ago, it seemed reasonable to predict that men and women were becoming more alike as traditional gender career pathways merged. It was a good guess that we would see the Sensitive New Age Guy (SNAG) nodding in deference before the CNAW, the Competent New Age Woman. It was a safe bet that the millennial generation, with their working mothers, cross-gender friendships, and coed bathrooms, would complete the revolution by overturning gender typecasting.

Instead, with the coming of the child-man, we've got a new version of the separate spheres. What gives? Why aren't young men evolving into postfeminist mensches? Let us count the reasons: demographic, economic, technological, cultural—and hormonal.

We've already had a glimpse of the demographic piece of this story. Men, like women, are taking longer to finish their educations, longer to get settled in their careers, and longer to get married and become fathers. The mean age of marriage, according to the Census Bureau, is now 28, up from 23.2 in 1970. In less than a decade, a remarkably short period for a shift of this sort, it rose more than a year—from 26.8 in 2000 to 28.1 in 2009.[2] In states with high numbers of college-educated men, such as New York, New Jersey, and Massachusetts, men stay single until they're 30.[3]

This means the emergence of a new and impressively large demographic group hanging out mostly in metropolitan areas and in no hurry to change their status: single young males—SYMs as marketers put it—between the ages of 18 and 34. SYMs have always existed, of course, but now they dominate the ranks of the twentysomethings. Consider the hordes of them implied by these numbers: In 1970, 80 percent of 25- to 29-year-old men were married; in 2007, only about 40 percent of them were. In 1970, 85 percent of 30- to 34-year-old men were married; in 2007, only 60 percent of them were.[4] That's a lot of men blissfully free of mortgages, wives, child-care bills, and—as we'll see, this is hugely important—biological clocks.

Recognizing the growing number and buying potential of SYMs in the 1990s, marketers, ad people, media execs, and cultural entrepreneurs began studying how to get them to commit—to their products. In the past, they hadn't been very successful. Young men were notoriously immune to the pleasures of magazines and television, as well as to the shopping expeditions that would lead them to the products advertised there. They were slackers when it came to buying stuff, so much so that the word "elusive" seemed permanently affixed to the phrase "men between 18 and 34" among advertisers. But by the mid-1990s, two things occurred that helped change that: first, cable television and the Internet fragmented the media audience, and second, with increasing media competition, the last vestiges of bourgeois reticence in entertainment began to give way. For marketers wanting to entice young men, the time was ripe.

Perhaps the signal moment arrived in April 1997, when Maxim, one of several popular "lad magazines" in England, arrived on American shores. Maxim purposely set out to be the anti–Playboy and Esquire; bad boy owner Felix Dennis sniffed at the idea of celebrity publishers with their formulas and philosophies about what men want. Instead, as editor Keith Blanchard later told a Columbia School of Journalism audience, the magazine's creators adopted the "astonishing methodology of asking our readers what they wanted . . . and then supplying it."[5]

And what did the desired reader—male, unmarried, median age 26, median household income $60,000 or so—want? Well, it wasn't Proust. Maxim plastered its covers and features with pouty-lipped, tousled-haired pinups in lacy underwear and, in case that didn't do the trick, big, neon-colored promises of Sex! Lust! Sexiest! Hottest!

Naughty! Customers lined up as if they were extras in a sequel of *Invasion of the Body Snatchers*. More than any other men's magazine before or since, *Maxim* captured the once-elusive 18–34 single, college-educated guy market with about 2.5 million readers, more than *GQ*, *Esquire*, and *Men's Journal* combined.[6]

Victoria's Secret cover art was not the entire key to *Maxim*'s success; after all, while until its arrival *Esquire* and GQ largely relied on male celebrities or Armani-clothed models to sell their mags, plenty of other down-market venues had the sort of bodacious covers bound to raise the testosterone level of the young male consumer. No, what set *Maxim* apart from other men's mags was its voice. It was the sound of guys hanging around the Animal House living room—where put-downs are high-fived; gadgets are cool; rock stars, sports heroes, and cyborg battles are awesome; jobs and Joni Mitchell suck; and girls are simply hot—or not.

In other words, *Maxim* asked the SYM what he wanted and got this answer: he wanted to hear he didn't have to grow up. He wanted to be a child-man. Whatever else you want to say about *Playboy* and *Esquire*, they tried to project the image of an intelligent, cultured, and au courant sort of man. As Hugh Hefner famously, and from today's cultural vantage point, risibly, wrote in one of his magazine's first issues, his ideal reader enjoyed "inviting a female acquaintance in for a quiet discussion of Picasso, Nietzsche, jazz, sex." *Playboy* had its famous *Playboy* philosophy; it may not have been Aristotle, but it did represent an attempt of sorts to define the good life. This kind of stuff would make the *Maxim* dude want to hurl. He would like to forget he ever went to school. For that matter, he'd like to forget he ever learned how to read.[7] *Maxim* editors do all they can to oblige. Reading *Maxim*, something that more than 2.5 million (mostly) men continued to do in 2009,[8] leaves the impression that child-men like lists almost as much as hot women: Twenty People We'd Hate to Have Dinner With, Ten Greatest Video Game Heroes of All Time, The Five Unsexiest Women Alive, Sixteen People Who Look Like They Absolutely Reek, and so forth. True, they publish actual articles, such as "Confessions of a Strip Club Bouncer," but they rely so much on picture-laden service features promoting the latest in skateboards, video games, and camcorders, with the occasional Q and A with Kid Rock, that they end up producing the bare minimum of print required to keep a magazine from being labeled a shopping catalogue or pinup calendar.

It's easy enough to sneer at all of this, but *Maxim*, like many other popular child-man amusements, is far from dumb. Not only has it made its creators a lot of money, it has helped to define a new male persona, such as it is. The child-man prides himself on his lack of pretense, his slovenly guyness, not to mention his fascination with bodily fluids and noises. The child-man is the reason, for instance, for the success of iFart, an iPhone app—in fact, "The Premier iPhone Fart Application"—that imitates the noise suggested by its name. (On April Fool's Day, 2010, the company issued a press release about its new "olfactic framework" that releases scents through the iPhone speaker.) At the same time, it's important to recognize that the child-man knows very well he is playing to clownish sociological type. In *Maxim* and other child-man outlets, sentences seem crowded with ironic quotation marks as if to announce, "We seem like just a bunch of horny, stupid, insensitive guys, but we don't take ourselves too seriously. You shouldn't either." The title of a *Maxim* article, "How to Make Your Girlfriend Think Her Cat's Death Was an Accident," for instance, contains just the right amount of callousness and misogyny to be naughty without being menacing. The editors position themselves the same way when they grumble about the popular (with women) show *Grey's Anatomy:* "The only thing worse than a show about doctors is a show about sappy chick doctors we're forced to watch or else our girlfriends won't have sex with us."

Television executives figured out a similar formula to attract the SYM viewer. Only fifteen years ago, television was largely a no–young man's land. Apart from sports events; *The Simpsons,* which was first broadcast in 1989; and four ESPN channels, there wasn't much to make child-men pick up the remote. Most prime-time television appealed to women and families, whose sensibilities are as alien to dudes as finger bowls. Jimmy Jellinek, who left as editor in chief at *Maxim* before taking the helm at Heavy.com (the semiotics of male media is a rich topic of its own), chided the media for their perennial complaints about the lack of "young male eyeballs"; television has "little in the way of mindless action, gratuitous bikini shots and talking cars," he explained. If there were, "maybe . . . we'd start watching TV again."

The suits at Comedy Central were among the first to see the wisdom of Jellinek's complaint. In its infancy in the early 1990s, Comedy Central had relied on movie comedies and stand-up acts, neither of which resulted in much success. The following several years brought the network some buzz with such shows as *Politically Incorrect* and the cartoon series *Dr. Katz, Professional Therapist,* but it was in 1997 that the network struck gold after it launched a cartoon series starring a group of foul-mouthed eight-year-old boys. With its relentlessly foul subversion of politesse, *South Park,* as the series was called, was like a dog whistle that only SYMs could hear; thanks largely to them, the show became a smash hit.

In 1999, the network followed up with *The Man Show,* famous for its Juggies (half-naked women with exceptionally large . . . well, juggies), interviews with porn stars, drinking songs, and an opening jingle that included the advice, "Quit your job and light a fart / Yank your favorite private part." "If Maxim were TV, it would be 'The Man Show,'" one reviewer said.[9] The founding fathers of *The Man Show*, Jimmy Kimmel and Adam Carolla, both went on to bring the child-man sensibility into the mainstream. Kimmel now has his own late-night television show, and Carolla has become an Internet entrepreneur, launching a podcast show that was downloaded 50 million times in 2009 and named best audio podcast of that year by iTunes.[10] Comedy Central's viewers, about 64 percent of whom are men, most of them young,[11] have also launched the careers of such male stars as Dave Chappelle, Lewis Black, Daniel Tosh, Stephen Colbert, and, most notably, Jon Stewart, *The Daily Show*'s anchor, all of whom, if not child-men exactly, project much of the requisite goofy edginess. (The network also produced three seasons of *The Sarah Silverman Program*, starring the only child-woman of any note; evidently, the female version didn't appeal to enough viewers because the show was canceled in 2010.)

Other executives created entire new networks for the viewing pleasure of the discriminating child-man. The G4 Channel is devoted to gaming and Internet news; BlackBelt TV broadcasts martial arts 24 hours a day. One of the most successful guy channels, Spike, came on the air in its current guise in 2003 with wrestling matches, reruns of *Star Trek*, and the high-tech detective drama *CSI*. It also created original shows, such as *Babe Hunt*, in which contestants try to detect the differences in two almost identical pictures of nearly naked women. Another show, *1,000 Ways to Die*, began to feature dramatizations of weird real-life accidents (example: a drunk driver leaning his head out the window to vomit is decapitated when he passes a mailbox). Several years ago, the Cartoon Network also spied the potential in the child-man market and introduced Adult Swim, late-night programming with such adult cartoons as *Family Guy*, whose superstar auteur, Seth

McFarlane, is himself a single, thirtysomething sci fi fan; *Boondocks*; and *Futurama*, a cult favorite cocreated by Matt Groening of *The Simpsons* fame. Adult Swim cut into the Letterman and Leno audience, luring a lot of gold-plated advertisers, including Saab, Apple, and Taco Bell;[12] child-men, it should come as no surprise, eat a lot of fast food.

By the mid- to late 1990s, movie producers also went on a child-man binge, producing so many dumb and dumber movies for them that Hollywood productions seemed to segregate into what the *New York Times* called Guy Land and Gal Land. ("In Gal Land clothes are made to be put on; in Guy Land they're made to be taken off.")[13] Adam Sandler is only one of the Guy Land stars. Also joining the toga party are Jim Carrey and "The Frat Pack," the group of twenty- and thirtysomething male comedians including Will Ferrell, Ben Stiller, Vince Vaughan, Owen and Luke Wilson, Steve Carrell, and, depending on which expert you listen to, Jack Black. The first Frat Pack movies, *Bottle Rocket* and *The Cable Guy*, arrived in 1996. The genre went on to include *There's Something About Mary*, *Meet the Parents*, *Zoolander*, *Anchorman*, *Dodgeball*, and the Judd Apatow creations, including *The 40 Year Old Virgin* and what might be considered the child-man national anthem, *Knocked Up*. With a talent for crude physical comedy, gleeful juvenility, and self-humiliation, these guys are the child-man counterpart to smoother, more conventional romantic leads, such as George Clooney and Brad Pitt, beloved by women and *Esquire* editors. The Frat Pack are particularly gifted at the gross-out humor involving embarrassing bodily parts that SYMs can't get enough of. In the 2003 *Old School*, three guys in their thirties decide to start a college fraternity. Frank the Tank (the moniker refers to his capacity for alcohol) is played by Will Ferrell, who flashes his saggy white derriere when he streaks through the college town; the scene is a child-man classic.

Nothing attests to the SYM's growing economic and cultural muscle more than video games. Once upon a time, video games were for little boys (and to a lesser extent, girls) who loved their Nintendos so much, it was widely lamented, they were no longer going outside to play ball or build forts. Today, those boys have grown up to become child-man gamers, turning a once niche industry into a more than $10 billion media powerhouse; insiders brag that their yearly intake has well surpassed Hollywood box office receipts.[14] Men between the ages of 18 and 34 are now the biggest users of video games; according to Nielsen Media's "The State of the Console," a study of video game use in the last quarter of 2006, almost half—48.2 percent—of 18- to 34-year-old American men had used a console and did so on average *2 hours and 43 minutes per day*. (That's 13 minutes more than 12- to 17-year-olds, who have either more responsibilities or at least adults determined to pull the plug.)[15] Now it is online gaming that is the next big thing; *World of Warcraft*, the biggest sensation, claims ten million subscribers worldwide, two and a half million of them in North America.[16] Until the recent arrival of social networks, gaming, both the games themselves and news and information about games, registered as the top category in monthly surveys of Internet usage. Today it is number two and still represents more than 10 percent of the hours spent on the Internet in the United States.[17]

Indeed, the child-man's home sweet media home is the Internet, where no meddling censor or nervous advertiser can come between him and his desires. Some sites, such as MensNews Daily.com, are edgy news sites with men in mind. Others, most notably AskMen.com, which claims five million visitors a month, resemble *Maxim*, which also has a website. AskMen has a feature called The Player, with articles titled "How to Score a Masseuse," "How to Score a Cop," and "How to Score with a Green Chick" that are in the best spirit of *Maxim*-style near-self-parody. "How is an SUV-driving, to-go-cup using, walking environmental catastrophe like yourself supposed to hook up with them?" the article asks. Answer: go to environmental meetings, yoga classes, or progressive bookstores ("but watch out for lesbians") and carry reusable cloth bags.

But there are other sites, Menarebetterthanwomen.com, The Best Page in the Universe, and Drunkasaurusrex.com, for instance, that walk *Maxim*'s good-natured woman-teasing over the line into a pure misogyny that would have a hard time convincing Taco Bell to come on board. The men who hang out on these sites take pride in being "badasses" (the brothers—or are they soul mates?— of the "badass" women we saw in Chapter 2) and stew in their bitterness toward the "other half." A misogynist is a "man who hates women as much as women hate each other," writes one poster at menarebetterthanwomen. Another who calls himself Monkeyman rails about "classic woman 'trap' questions—Does this make me look fat? Which one of my friends would you sleep with if you had to? Do you really enjoy strip clubs?" The Fifth Amendment was created because its architects' wives "drove them ape-shit asking questions that they'd be better off simply refusing to answer."

Contemporary undomesticated SY maledom appears in its darkest form in the person of Tucker Max, whose eponymous website is a great favorite among his peers. To anyone thinking that the child-man is just a dumb C student, his résumé will come as a surprise. In a previous age, Max would have been what was known as "a catch." Good-looking, ambitious, and smart, he graduated from the University of Chicago and Duke Law School. He has found it more to his liking—and remarkably easy—to take up a career path outside the law in more ways than one: professional "asshole." Max writes, or says he writes, "true stories about my nights out acting like an average twentysomething"—binge drinking (Urbandictionary.com lists "Tucker Max Drunk," or TMD, as a synonym for "falling down drunk"); fighting; leaving vomit and fecal detritus for others to clean up; and most of all, hooking up with scores of "random" girls—"slutty" UNC or UVA sorority sisters, Vegas waitresses, Dallas lap dancers, and Junior Leaguers into erotic asphyxiation.

Crudity is at the heart of the child-man persona—the bad-boy tone epitomizes his refusal to grow up—but Max takes this boorishness to its pathological limit. Throughout his adventures, Max remains fixated on his penis and his "dumps," like a toddler stuck somewhere around the oedipal stage. He is utterly without conscience: "Female insecurity: it's the gift that keeps on giving," he writes about his efforts to undermine his prey's self-esteem in order to seduce them. Think of Max as the last spawn of an aging and chromosomally challenged Hugh Hefner, and of his website and best-selling book, *I Hope They Serve Beer in Hell*, as evidence of a male culture in profound decline. In Freudian terms, *Playboy's* aspirations toward cultivation and refinement hinted at the continuing call of the ego and a culture with limits on male restiveness; Max, the child-man who answers to no one except his fellow "assholes," is all id—and proud of it.

That sound you hear? That's women not laughing. Oh, some of them get a kick out of child-men and their frat/fart jokes; *Maxim* has claimed that more than 20 percent of its readers are female,[18] for instance, and it's reasonable to suppose that not all of them are doing R&D for the dating scene. But many members of the New Girl Order, understandably put off by Juggies and exploding toilets, blame the media for the child-man in their midst.[19] They're right to this extent: pop culture is more than occasional entertainment for this population. It is the oxygen they breathe. In *About a Boy*, Nick Hornby—a British novelist and one of the shrewdest child-man observers—writes about his 36-year-old slacker hero: "Sixty years ago, all the things Will relied on to get him through the day simply didn't exist: there was no daytime TV, there were no videos, there were no glossy magazines . . . and there were probably no record shops. . . . Now, though, it was easy [to not work]. There was almost too much to do."[20] Will, whose name is a joke because he has so little of it, has no self apart from pop culture effluvia, a fact the author symbolizes by having him live off the residuals of a popular Christmas song written by his late father.

Still, blaming the media doesn't make much sense. Media execs just want to find an audience; they make dumb Adam Sandler movies and Super Bowl ads because that's how they can lock those eyeballs. They can't foist a new cultural type on an unwilling public. Media executives didn't *invent* the child-man; they *uncovered* him. So the question is: how did the child-man get inside the contemporary SYM?

The most prevalent theory comes from feminist-influenced academics and cultural critics. In a series of books and articles published in the 1990s, these writers argued that men were suffering a "crisis of masculinity" taking the form of a defensive backlash against feminist gains. Threatened by women's empowerment and in an age of downsizing, manufacturing decline, and the erosion of the living wage, men were "cling[ing] desperately to outdated roles," in the words of prominent theorist Susan Faludi in her 1991 book titled, simply, *Backlash*. Faludi followed up with *Stiffed* in 1999, in many respects a more sympathetic treatment of men, but one that nevertheless posited that they grow up believing they are "going to be the master of the universe and all that was in it."[21]

Their disappointment with their downsized fate, she concludes, drives them to macho displays.

In his 2008 *Guyland: The Perilous World Where Boys Become Men*, the gender studies sociologist Michael Kimmel applied Faludi's reading of the masculinity crisis specifically to young men. In Kimmel's view, today's young men have "a privileged sense that they are special, that the world is there for them to take." To maintain their status among the entitled, they follow the "Guy Code," a set of behaviors that include "never showing emotions or admitting to weakness," ridiculing homosexuals, and trying to "have sex with as many women as possible."[22]

There is an element of truth to some of this. The child-man is preoccupied with sex, though it's hard to see how he is distinguishing himself from other young males of any species or any culture in this regard. It is also true that some child-men are openly in backlash mode, though they would argue it is less out of resentment of women's success than out of a belief that feminist media gatekeepers—that is, agents, editors, producers, and the like—don't understand or accept the appeal of real guy stuff. They know they are violating widely accepted feminist rules about the way men ought to behave, and they gleefully stick their thumbs in the eyes of those they view as politically correct tsk-tskers. In one episode of *South Park*, for instance, the Sexual Harassment Panda, a mascot who teaches schoolkids the evils of sexual harassment, is fired after his lectures lead to a flood of inane lawsuits.

But the backlash interpretation falters in the face of several facts. For one thing, the idea that boys today are especially anxious about homosexuality when they have grown up with gay pride parades, LGBT clubs, and *Brokeback Mountain* squares with neither common sense nor surveys showing millennials favoring gay rights, including gay marriage, by large margins.[23] For another, it's hard to see where these guys might have gotten the idea that they would be twenty-first-century overlords. The college-educated inhabitants of Kimmel's Guyland never knew a world where women weren't lawyers and managers or where slayers named Buffy didn't take care of the vampires. Hey, they loved the Powerpuff Girls as much as their sisters did, maybe more.[24] Nor are they smarting because they were stiffed by changes in the labor market. As we've seen, the work possibilities of college-educated men improved substantially over the past thirty years—and so did their wages.[25]

There's also the fact that the child-man comes in a number of guises, some of them bearing little resemblance to the troglodytes of the backlash imagination. This is a point worth considering for a moment to dispel any easy assumption that the child-man is simply a Sigma Phi Epsilon stuck in a time warp and to illustrate just how widespread the cultural shift he represents has been. Take the child-men usually referred to as "geeks" and "nerds." The geek is primarily known for his obsession with all things computer, though he is mesmerized by other gadgets, games, and esoteric heavy metal bands as well. He tends to systematize reality in ways that can be bizarre to nongeeks. His close cousin, the nerd, is also brainy but tends to be a little less mechanical in his approach to things. With a passion for sci fi and fantasy, he collects comics, although given that he has committed vast sections of Tolkien to memory, you have to admit he has a literary side as well. He likes "nerdcore" bands who rap about *Star Wars*. Both geeks and nerds tend to be socially maladroit and hold attitudes toward the "second sex" that are more reminiscent of the junior high school band than the college Animal House. See, for example, Steve Carrell's character in *The 40 Year Old Virgin*, a child-man who collects large action figures, not notches on his bedpost.

Another genus in the child-man taxonomy is the emo-boy. Unlike most of their peers, emo-boys like talking about their feelings. They are often handsome in a scruffy, boyish way (think Kurt Cobain). By contemporary standards, they are somewhat cultured, with a taste in obscure indie bands (some spy the origins of the emo-boy in the Seattle grunge movement of the 1990s) and novels about male alienation. One of the most well reviewed of those novels was Benjamin Kunkel's 2005 novel *Indecision*, whose 28-year-old hero suffers from a rare illness called "abulia," defined—here comes that theme again—by a lack of will or initiative. Unfortunately, according to the women who pass through his life, the emo-boy's vulnerability and soulful conversation are ultimately indistinguishable from his childish self-regard and hopeless incompetence.[26] The writer Katie Roiphe discovered something similar in the novels of young male writers, including Kunkel: "Passivity, a paralyzed sweetness, a deep ambivalence about sexual appetite, are somehow taken as signs of a complex and admirable inner life," she writes. "Even the mildest display of male aggression is a sign of being overly hopeful, overly earnest or politically untoward."[27]

Consider the actor Jason Schwartzman, the iconic emo-boy. In the television series *Bored to Death*, he plays a lost twenty-something who, after his girlfriend leaves him, pretends, with modest success, to be a private detective. In *Darjeeling Limited*, he is one of three child-man brothers on a trek to find their long-lost mother. Along the way, his character hooks up with an Indian train stewardess. Puzzled by his odd persona, she asks, "What's wrong with you?" He pauses before answering, "Let me think about that."

If this were real life, he probably wouldn't do that. The child-man is not known for serious self-reflection, and even if he had the impulse to think about how to invest his energies in things that really matter, he would have trouble knowing how. As we're about to see, television, magazines, and games are not the only, and maybe not even the major, way culture tells the child-man that not much is expected of him.

five

FATHER OF CHILD-MAN

The child-man may be a cultural figure unique to our time, but he didn't jump fully formed from the brains of Felix Dennis and Judd Apatow, like Athena from the head of Zeus. In fact, he has a long and perhaps not entirely distinguished ancestry going back more than a century. Still one thing above all separates his forefathers from him: they knew they were going to be tied to, and responsible for, a family. He does not.

This may sound suspiciously like family values agitprop, but it is nevertheless true: adult manhood has almost universally been equated with marriage and fatherhood. The life script for most men was pretty simple: you're born; you grow up; you learn to do the hunting, fishing, building, farming, and the like expected of you; you get married; you have children; you get old (if you're lucky); and you die. There were exceptions. In polygamous societies, low-status men often had neither wives nor children; in others, some men became priests, and some soldiers. And of course, there was a wide range of marital ideals; some cultures encouraged wife control through periodic beatings; others made heroes of Mr. Mom. Despite the variations, we can make several generalizations. First, men were required to provide, or help provide, for their wives and children, and in many cases for other family members. Second, in the face of danger, they had to protect these others as well. This is why so many premodern cultures had initiation rituals testing a boy's courage, perseverance, and competence. Most societies needed to ensure that come times of peril, their men would have the right stuff.[1]

Yet, as the anthropologist David Gilmore discovered in his study of manhood across cultures, even as societies have modernized, tribal definitions of masculinity maintained their hold on the human imagination. "At all levels of sociocultural development," Gilmore writes, "men who hunted and fished, men who farmed or made shoes, men who were lawyers or clerks . . . manhood is problematic, a critical threshold for boys to pass through."[2] In the story of masculinity told across cultures, the same qualities come up over and over: strength, courage, resolve, and sexual potency. Modernity—specifically urbanization and industrialization— should have reduced these warrior-like virtues to irrelevancy; butchers and grocers made hunting and fishing passé except as sport, and police and armies provided protection from dangers. Instead, as historians have frequently noted, industrialization invented the separation of male and female spheres (though not the separation of male and female labor, which were everywhere and always) and only reinforced conventional notions of masculinity and femininity. In the new regime, the home was women's territory, child-centered and nurturing; the public realm, all rough-and-tumble competition, was for men.

At least that's the way the story is usually told. But it's only partially correct. The separate spheres also worked toward domesticating middle-class men, forcing them to give up ancient male predilections, a project that provoked both pleasure and resistance in its subjects. Middle-class workers going to the office may have spent far more time away from their children than dads in the past, but they were expected to bring home a spirit of affection and playfulness that would have scandalized their own patriarchal fathers.[3] By the early years of the nineteenth century in England, according to the historian John Tosh, patriarchal aloofness was out of style on the home front. As the middle-class home became increasingly child-centered, both women and men were expected to project warmth, nurturing, and gentleness. However, men were not entirely at ease with the new emotional style. Restless and more than a little bored, they went looking for excitement and male camaraderie in empire-building, adventure novels by such authors as Robert Louis Stevenson, or going to "the club."[4]

By the latter part of the nineteenth century, American men were feeling similarly ambivalent about an increasingly cozy and refined domestic life. At the time, the United States was still primarily a rural nation, but growing numbers of young, unmarried men began to move to cities to find work in the new businesses sprouting up in the growing economy. These "bachelors," as they came to be known, had their pick of a wide variety of new entertainments—dance halls, billiard parlors, vaudeville theaters, and the like. Life was pretty good for what we might call ur-child-men, enough so that by 1890, marriage rates had declined dramatically and the median age of marriage for men—26.1—had temporarily reached what would be its highest level until the late twentieth century.[5]

Still, with a limited number of respectable women hanging around the billiard halls and, in any case, fairly strict rules against sex unless you put a ring on a finger, the vast majority of men—90 percent—would soon enough become husbands. As married men, they could no longer pursue most of their city bachelor pleasures; despite the separation of the spheres, men were not supposed to go to the pub after a day at the office. They were expected to give themselves over to domestic life. And so, like their English counterparts, they sought outlets for primordial virile urges that sat comfortably in the bourgeois parlor. They turned to the immensely popular *National Police Gazette*, with its sensational crime stories and articles about sports. Later came such titles as *Field and Stream* and *Action Stories*, as well as steamier fare, such as *Escapade* and *Caper*.[6] Men's adventure magazines (*Man's Exploits*, *Real Men*) continued to sell well into the middle of the twentieth century, though college-educated men, as we'll see in a moment, were moving their attention to the more sophisticated pleasures of *Esquire* and *Playboy*.[7]

Adding to male restiveness were changes in the nature of work. At the beginning of the nineteenth century, the large majority of men worked for themselves, mostly as farmers but also as tradesmen and small merchants. But by the end of the century, two-thirds were working for "the man" in factories or offices.[8] More and more, upwardly aspiring men found themselves spending their days sitting at desks, yes-ing the boss, dotting bureaucratic i's and crossing managerial t's. As women moved into clerical positions around the turn of the twentieth century and a little later even into professional positions, the office guy worked in an increasingly genteel environment. No swearing, dirty jokes, spitting—spittoons disappeared from offices during these years. Over time, carpets, plants, and paintings added to the domestic atmosphere.[9] Even away from home, it seemed, men couldn't escape the stuffy parlor.

By the 1920s, the corporate workplace was also becoming infused with a feminized therapeutic style. According to the sociologist Eva Illouz, new management theories of the time, heavily influenced by psychoanalysis, placed increasing emphasis on "at-

tention to emotions, controlling anger, and listening sympatheti-
cally to others." Where the Victorians had held to a belief in separate emotional styles as well as separate spheres, the twentieth
century "slowly eroded and reshuffled these boundaries by making emotional life central to the workplace."[10]

And so, a lot of men decided to go looking for some fresh air.
American men began to take a keen interest in competitive ath-
letics, the Western frontier, and the rugged outdoors. These were
the years that professional and college football and baseball became the national pastimes they remain today.[11] The Boy Scouts,
created in 1912, were designed to introduce overcivilized boys to
the thrill of the wild. Was this a misogynistic rebellion, a symp-
tom of male anxiety, and a way of protecting male turf, as contemporary historians often describe it? Sure, but that's hardly the
whole story. Young men of modernizing America weren't just dis-
tancing themselves from the female sphere; they didn't much care
for old-fashioned, overbearing male authority either. "The flight
from domesticity was as much a turning away from patriarchy as
from femininity," Tosh explains.[12] The truth is these men didn't
cotton to any of the many reformers of the turn of the century
who would tell them to behave themselves: purity crusaders, anti-
boxing activists, prohibitionists, sentimentalists, and moralists of
all stripes, secular or religious, female or male.[13]

Yet for all his annoyance with Victorian stuffiness and bourgeois refinement, the late nineteenth- and early twentieth-
century man resembled his forefathers in one major respect: his
primary adult duty was—or would be, if he was still a bachelor—
as husband and father to his wife and children. Just as anthropologists have found was the case throughout premodern cultures, so
it was for men of this era, and so it was for that matter well into

the twentieth century. Men knew this to be the defining aspect of mature manhood. Yes, everyone from the nineteenth-century paterfamilias to the 1950s Levittown, Long Island, dad chafed against the duties and responsibilities of his sex through pop culture fantasies of adventures at sea, pinups, or sublimated war on the football field and boxing rings (a major reason dads were willing to plunk down the money for television sets when they first came on the market). Yet there was considerable social and economic pressure for them to be grown-ups. Whether lawyer or clerk, for that matter whether factory line worker or janitor cleaning bathrooms in a city office building, such as the one profiled by the sociologist Richard Sennett, a man "had one single and durable purpose, the service of his family."[14]

Until the middle of the twentieth century, that is. That is when the male service ethic first came under serious attack. The arrival of *Playboy* in 1953 was not just the temporary, if often irritating, escape via football games and adventure stories, it was an all-out rebellion against mid-century family life and middle-class requirements of marital duty. "All woman wants is security," an early *Playboy* article complained. "And she is perfectly willing to crush man's adventurous freedom-loving spirit to get it." The language was vaguely familiar, but the ultimate goal of relieving the male sex of adult manhood as it had been commonly understood was not. *Playboy* sneered at marriage as the enslavement of men— or worse: "Day after day, week after week, the American hubby is invited to attend his own funeral," one writer announced in a 1963 article.[15] To escape death, men would have to stay [play]boys. Up until that time, youth worship would have been seen as bizarre. Boys wanted to grow up in part because only men—think Don Draper—could smoke, drink, have sex, and look manly, but also because only men could make their mark on the world. "Maturity was not dull, but heroic," writes Barbara Ehrenreich in *The Hearts of Men*.[16]

The antiauthoritarianism of the 1960s also conspired to deconstruct mature manhood. Boomer men rebelled against the Vietnam War; they also fought with their Greatest Generation fathers, whom they viewed, in a replay of turn-of-the-century bachelors against Victorian patriarchs, as rigid, closed-minded, and inauthentic "suits." They insisted on a more open, looser, egalitarian, even vaguely feminine style, symbolized by their long hair and brightly colored clothing. Where their fathers had manned up for the sake of God, family, and country in combat neutrals, the younger generation embraced pleasure, both sexual and pharmaceutical, and hoped to die before they got old.

By the late 1960s and early 1970s, the duty ethic took another hit from a less predictable source. Unwittingly linking arms with *Playboy*, second-wave feminists announced that women, too, were no longer interested in male providers. From the perspective of many frustrated women, the male breadwinner role was the root of sexual inequality. It made women dependent on men. It gave men power in the public sphere that was unavailable to housebound women. It reduced women to their roles as Mrs. So and So and mother of Susie and Johnny So and So. Many feminists may simply have hoped to redefine marriage as an equal partnership between husbands and wives, one that would make space for dual breadwinners, dual nurturers, and dual housekeepers. But prominent activists rejected marriage, which they, like *Playboy*, described as "slavery." Actually, they went further. They rejected the entire notion of the interdependence of the sexes. Men were simply not essential in women's lives ("A woman needs a man like a fish needs a bicycle," was Gloria Steinem's later memorable statement on the subject). Intentionally or not, this turned out to mean they would be only bit players in the lives of their children.[17] As rates of single motherhood began to rise to unprecedented levels, it signaled the end of the historical/cultural consensus that men had a profound and essential social role as providers (whether in tandem with women or not), as protectors, as husbands, and as fathers.[18]

In fact, many of today's young men either grew up without a father or saw uncles, family friends, or neighbors become uncomfortable, occasional visitors in their onetime homes. Observant boys—and, yes, there are a few—might have also noticed that male-bashing had become the lingua franca of advertising and situation comedy; the guy who starts a fire while cooking dinner to be put out by his multitasking wife who is already ordering takeout, the crowded remedial classroom of low-IQ television dads from Homer Simpson to Ray Romano to Tim Allen. Meanwhile, by the 1990s, as we saw in Chapter 2, the entire culture became a you-go-girl cheering section. Dads and moms took their daughters to work and left their sons to come home after a dull day of school and play their video games.

The widespread cultural attack on older forms of manhood left men in a bind. If they projected too much self-confidence or assertiveness, they would be, at best, out of touch, and at worst, a complete joke. These days, Stephen Colbert's pompous, windbag persona on *The Colbert Report* is a nightly riff on this kind of outmoded masculinity and a warning to all men tempted to regress. Instead, men tried to cool down the masculine persona through youthful playfulness and coy hesitancy. "Me?" they seemed to say. "I'm not a man. I'm a *guy*." Gary Cross observes in his *Men to Boys: The Making of Modern Immaturity* that the difference between yesterday and today can be summed up as the distance between the debonair Cary Grant and the tousled and "befuddled" Hugh Grant.[19] Even 50- and 60-year-old men do their best to project the aura of a 25-year-old bad boy: Howard Stern, Don Imus, and all of the other radio shock jocks, as well as the impressive stable of boomer male rock stars with hip replacements and heart stents. Dave Barry, the youngest-looking 62-year-old man aside from Benjamin Button, publishes *I'll Mature When I'm Dead*, and it sells big time.

In the contemporary cultural environment, men have also had to reinvent fatherhood. Today, Cross notes, "a man can relate to a boy only by accentuating his own immaturity."[20] This explains the popularity of the Twitter feed made into a number-one best-selling book and TV series, *Shit My Father Says*. Writes Justin Halpern, a sometime *Maxim* contributor, on his website, "I'm 29. I live with my 74-year-old Dad. He is awesome. I just write down shit that he says." (A representative nugget of fatherly wisdom: "We're basically on earth to shit and fuck.") The writer Neal Pollack provides another example of fatherhood reimagined for today in his 2006 memoir *Alternadad*. Pollack struggles with his new role as father to Elijah, or, as he calls him, "the new roommate," until he finds he can introduce his toddler to the best alternative bands—"My son and I were moshing! Awesome!"—and realizes how many opportunities there are to engage his child-man fascination with poop.[21]

The child-man, then, is the lost son of a host of economic and cultural changes: the demographic shift I call preadulthood, the *Playboy* philosophy, feminism, the wild west of our new media, and a shrugging iffiness on the subject of husbands and fathers. He has no life script, no special reason to grow up. Of course, you shouldn't feel too bad for him; he's having a good enough time. But preening with a sense of entitlement he is not. In fact, after passing through boyhood and adolescence, he arrives at preadulthood with the distinct sense that he is dispensable, that being a guy is a little embarrassing and that given his social ambiguity, he might as well just play with the many toys (and babes—he hopes) his culture has generously provided him. After all, he is free as men have never been free before.

In this respect, he differs from his female peers. Women have the advantage, miserable as it sometimes makes them, of knowing about biological limits. The large majority of women want to have children, or so the surveys consistently say.[22] That means they will not be able to play—or work without serious distraction—for very long. Even those who are unsure whether they will have children know that the decision alone imposes boundaries on their pre-adulthood. There's a lot to get done before their ovaries begin to demand prompt attention. Young men, even the large majority who hope to have a family eventually, don't have this deadline. Those who are uncertain about domestic life: well, no one's going to miss them. Husbands and fathers are optional anyway.

It would be impossible to prove for certain that the loss of the almost universal male life script—manhood defined by marriage and fatherhood—is key to the mystery of the child-man. But there are a few studies suggesting that at the very least, young men who are married or who expect to marry are motivated to work harder and make more investments in their future and are less prone to substance abuse and unemployment. Eric Gould at the Hebrew University in Jerusalem looked at the schooling and career decisions of more than 2,000 young American men between ages 16 and 39. He concluded that if there were no returns to career choices in the marriage market, that is, if the type of career they chose, and their success at that career, didn't improve their chances of marrying a quality woman, "men would tend to work less, study less, and choose blue-collar jobs over white-collar jobs."[23] In other words, men succeed to prove themselves to potential partners. The study didn't look at the highest-achieving men, but it does help to explain some of the behavior of men who straddle blue- and white-collar worlds. Studies consistently find that married men earn more than single, divorced, and separated men. A common response to findings of this sort is that they are a product of self-selection: the men who make more money are the kind of men who marry.

It's not possible to answer that objection definitively, but researchers have come close. The sociologist Steven Nock, for instance, tracked a group of more than 5,000 men of a wide variety of ethnic, racial, regional, and class backgrounds over fifteen years. He found that their earnings increased an average of $4,000 annually after they married as compared with similar men who divorced, remarried, became widowed, or remained single. They work harder, and they are more likely to move up the career ladder when they are married. Interestingly, men who married for a second time showed none of these benefits; their hours of work, income, and job prestige actually declined. Nock speculates this is because a second marriage has no script telling men what's expected of them. Or perhaps, they just aren't going to try that hard the second time around.[24]

Of course, even child-men have to pay the rent, meaning they have to work. Life cannot be one long bachelor party. Yet, they might find the respectable, bureaucratized environments of the office irksome, just as men of the nineteenth century did. Strict sexual harassment codes and a mildly therapeutic emotional style that Eva Illouz has described as "cold intimacy" now color the corporate atmosphere.[25] The sort of emotional intelligence valued in many sectors of the knowledge economy is not generally the child-man's strong suit.

Happily, the knowledge economy has also carved out a variety of different SYM work ghettoes where the interests and personality of the child-man's home are prized and even nurtured. Trader rooms have long been child-man enclaves. (What's the difference between a bond and a bond trader? A bond matures, goes an old Wall Street joke.) Tech companies, of course, are a haven for geeky child-men. These offices reject the more formal, controlled personality of the lawyer or public relations executive. They provide environments meant to encourage playful innovativeness, including game rooms furnished with Ping-Pong tables—geeks evidently love Ping-Pong[26]—rock band equipment, video game consoles, foosball, and climbing walls. The explosion in entertainment media has also been a boon to the dude and nerd set. The gaming industry is a mecca for child-men looking for a cool career; one company alone, Blizzard Entertainment, employs 4,600 staffers just to work on *World of Warcraft*.[27] Assuming you aren't Jon Stewart or Jimmy Kimmel, if you are really, really lucky, you might work for them or others like them as a producer, writer, editor, or talent coordinator. There are few women working in the offices of these late-night comedians, and those who do describe a bantering, competitive, mocking atmosphere that doesn't differ much from guys hanging out with their friends in their walk-up apartments.[28]

The fratty child-man, the guy into sports and beer above all else, can also spend his time doing what he loves. He could work for ESPN or one of its twelve related channels, or the Golf, Tennis, Fox Soccer, NFL, NHL, or College Sports network. He could work for a business selling the sorts of consumer items he and his bros enjoy, or for that matter create his own business, like the successful inventor of iFart. As of 2010, according to the Association of Brewers, there were 1,558 "microbreweries." The growth in these small artisanal manufacturers of beer was exponential after 1990 with improved technology, communications, and distribution.[29] A while back, *Maxim* published a letter from a reader asking, "Are there any cool jobs related to beer?" Why, yes, young man; yes, there are. The editors list several, brand manager, beer tester, and brewmaster among them. We can hasten to add webmaster for such sites as Careersinbeer.com or Beertherapy.com. Artsier beer enthusiasts might dream of making Budweiser ads for Super Bowl halftime or maybe even a documentary like the 2004 *American Beer*. Fortysomething Steve Sheraton, of the Las Vegas–based software developer Hottrix, is a hero for many child-men. A self-described producer/inventor and trained magician, Sheraton created iBeer, an iPhone app that turns the screen into a frothy glass of beer you can pretend to chug.

Disapproval from some killjoy women aside, has there ever been a better time to be a guy? Don't be too sure. There are signs that the life of the child-man has its dangers. The sharpest of recent child-man entertainments, Judd Apatow's *Knocked Up*, offers some insight into signs of unease in the promised land. When the grubby, pot-headed, 23-year-old Ben Stone accidentally impregnates Alison, he is clueless about what to do when she decides to have the baby, not because he is a bad guy. No, he is just a big boy with a big heart. His problem is that he has grown up in a culture with no wisdom to offer about being a grown-up man, nothing to say about his obligations either to his future child or his child's mother. His father is useless: "I've been divorced three times," he tells Ben when his son asks for advice about his predicament. "Why are you asking me?" His roommates are useless; they spend their time squabbling about who farted on whose pillow and when to launch their porn website. In the end, despite the social retards in his midst, Ben tries to grow up; he gets a job and an apartment and becomes attached to Alison and the baby.

Of course, this is a comedy, or to be more precise a fairy tale for guys. You wouldn't know how to become an adult even if you wanted to? Maybe a beautiful, sweet princess will come along and show you. But probably not.

six

LOVE IN A
TIME OF DARWINISM

If she were alive today, how would Jane Austen begin her novel about preadults? "It is a truth universally acknowledged that a single man or woman in possession of a good diploma must be in want of . . ." In want of what exactly? A hook-up? A girlfriend or boyfriend? A long-term relationship (LTR, as it is noted in the personals)? A soul mate? A husband or wife? A surrogate womb? An apartment?

The long period of career and personal development that is preadulthood is a cultural artifact, a consequence of momentous economic and value shifts. It has much to recommend it. It allows the young to discover their talents and cultivate them, it treats women as equal in this task to men, and it prizes genuine achievement over bloodlines (though it unfortunately gets overly excited about credentials). But if preadulthood is an enlightened philosopher when it comes to work and self-fulfillment, it is a lazy mute when it comes to love, sex, and marriage. We've already seen that it's not sure what to make of men. Especially when it comes to dating, preadults are deeply ambivalent about how men are supposed to act. Caught between biology and culture—or is it past and future?—they date in a cultural vacuum that leaves fools, scoundrels, and louts to rush into the "meet market" and bedroom.

The cultural silence about dating and mating may not seem odd to avid individualists such as ourselves, but it is—very odd, and not because old people always try to prevent young people from having fun. Social groups have always taken a keen interest in the procreative activities of their younger, fertile members because they have a major stake in ensuring that the offspring of those fertile members will get what they need to become productive citizens. That's the primary reason that social groups have always set out clearly marked paths for sex, marriage, and parenthood. Chaos was the alternative: single mothers dependent on who knows whom, abandoned and neglected children, siblings with varied fathers, ambiguous paternity, jealous passions, men without clear bonds and obligations.

For a variety of reasons, traditional societies not only provided a script for the young to follow as they made their way to marriage and parenthood. They also gave strict orders, or at a minimum careful guidance, about who would marry (which added up to sleeping with) whom, and about which men would be official father to which women's children. We may view sexual freedom and a soul mate as our birthright, but in most cases in the civilized record, couples were either forced or pushed into unions about which they had little or no say. To this day, arranged marriages are the norm in South Asia and the Middle East, and forced marriages remain commonplace in parts of Africa, Afghanistan, Pakistan, and Bangladesh. Immigrants from these areas often carry their customs to England, France, and other European countries, much to the distress of the local populace.

That's because here in the Western world, couples have long had a choice in matters of the heart. Yes, there was always a good deal of adult supervision in the form of chaperones, church dances, community socials, and curfews, as well as structural limitations like a dearth of privacy and residential immobility. For much of American history, single men and women lived under the rule of "family government"—residing with family members and in need of their support—enough so that while in theory they were free to marry whom they wanted, in practice they didn't have all that much choice.[1] It was only in the twentieth century, when Americans introduced the custom of dating and gained access to the automobile—a "whorehouse on wheels" according to some worriers in the early twentieth century—that young people gained some freedom from disapproving adult eyes. Even in that case, communities were small and cohesive enough that the same rules tended to be internalized by every middle-class, or aspiring middle-class, man and woman: a man was supposed to call a woman for a date; he was supposed to pick up his date; he was supposed to take his date out, say, to a dance, a movie, or an ice cream joint; he was supposed to try to entice her into sex; and at some point if the relationship seemed charged enough—or if she got pregnant—he was supposed to ask her to marry him.

Today, of course, there are no parents, ministers, rabbis, priests, or matchmakers telling the young whom not to have sex with or whom to marry or when. Financially and sexually independent, both men and women have escaped dating rituals, rules, and gender roles. They're free to do whatever they want, and their opportunities for pursuing happiness on their own terms are like none before in human experience. They can marry the first girl or guy they met in college, to whom they have been entirely faithful.

They can dally with one hundred men or women (or both); consider one Harvard-educated New Yorker named Paul Janka who in a web post in 2007 announced that he had made a—forgive me—spreadsheet of his hundred-plus partners to determine whether having dinner or drinks was more likely to lead women to have sex with him. (Answer: it's not dinner.)[2] Preadults can—and most seem to—sow a few wild oats in their twenties and then find a soul mate with whom they plan an artisanal wedding in their parents' backyard—or a multiday blowout in a villa in Italy. They can travel the world and find lovers in every port. They can marry their true love at 24 and divorce him or her at 25. They can live with their boyfriend or girlfriend and then get married. Or they can break up with them and live with someone else. They can take up polyamory. They can decide they like living alone and get a cat.

So let's consider how that freedom plays out on the ground. A guy walks into a bar, or for that matter a party or bowling alley. A girl catches his eye, holds it a minute, and looks down with a barely detectable blush in her cheeks. The gesture is a universal signal of romantic interest, understood by men from Brazil to Bangladesh, but in the present circumstances our SYM has to figure out what "romantic interest" means. For an idea of the range of possible interpretations, consider this post on Jezebel, a popular website for young women: "I've gone through phases in my life where I bounce between serial monogamy, Very Serious Relationships and extremely casual sex. I've slept next to guys on the first date, had sex on the first date, allowed no more than a cheek kiss, dispensed with the date-concept all together [sic] after kissing the guy on the way to his car, fucked a couple of close friends and, more rarely, slept with a guy I didn't care if I ever saw again."[3] Some men might think that if a woman spends the night with him, even if it is after a half-dozen shots of tequila, she's actually interested in him. That's one way of thinking about it, but many women think casual sex is a lame way to start a LTR. For them, a hook-up might mean the opposite—namely, that they expect to blot the whole night from their memory. In other words, freedom turns out to be just another word for nothing left to assume. It doesn't help that our young bar hopper may be a child-man. Dating rules of the *Mad Men* era had any number of problems, not the least being its adherents' tendency to end up in a tract house with an unhealthy fondness for gin and tranquilizers. The upside was that anybody with an emotional IQ over 70 could follow the rules. To navigate today's mating scene and to read all of those unspoken messages—about how things are going; whether she thinks you're coming across as too strong or too lame; whether she's got a drinking problem or is just really thirsty; whether you detected a note of regret when she told that story about her ex-boyfriend; whether she's coming back to your apartment because it's easier than saying no, because she's lonely, or because she thinks you're hot—a guy must be an Einstein of emotional intelligence. Child-men, as we've seen, are somewhere on the downside of the bell curve, and even those with high EQ potential may not care to use it as long as they can find women willing to have sex with them.

Those on the geeky side are more likely to have a statistically significant EQ learning disability. Because of their technical skills, geeks often have good jobs, nice apartments, and a sober demeanor; they seem like they could make good boyfriends. But they are prone to the sort of hyper-methodical obsessions that is poison to flirting and seduction. In 2004, *Wired* profiled Chau Vuong, the 33-year-old author of a popular Internet pamphlet, *The Soul Mate Manifesto*, who is trying to find "a mathematical model that could predict and explain all human behavior pertaining to love." As for his own personal life: "I don't actually date. I research it." Vuong is a brilliant, successful, single young man with a lively mind, but his programmer instincts have kept him a virgin. "If I was a tall, good-looking white guy, I'd be on *The Bachelor*," he sighs. "But I'll never make it on there. I'm a nerdy, short Asian guy."[4] (More on the overall plight of Asian guys coming up.)

Women are equally perplexed. A girl walks into a bar. A guy gives her the once-over. Is he only interested in one thing, as the old saying used to go? Or is he soul mate material? Is he looking for a friends-with-benefits arrangement or for romance? He could have a girlfriend, a wife, an ex-wife, children, or a spreadsheet. Does he like women or is he gay? Worse, is he one of those guys so filled with bitterness that he hangs around websites like Nomarriage.com, MGTOW (Men Going Their Own Way), or EternalBachelor ("Give Modern Women the Husband They Deserve. None.")? In small communities, a girl either knew a man's family or people who knew his family or someone who had worked with his brother or people who went to college with his sister or *something*.[5] In the anonymous canyons of the preadult city, the guy is a stranger, and possibly even strange. Men sometimes complain that women are always saying, "What are you thinking?" Under the circumstances, you can't really blame them for asking.

Women often find they are talking a different language, both literal and figurative, from the men they meet. "Recently my mother asked me to clarify what I meant when I said I was dating someone, versus when I was hooking up with someone, versus when I was seeing someone," began a much-discussed *New York Times* article titled "Want to Be My Boyfriend? Please Define." "And I had trouble answering her because the many options overlap and blur in my mind."[6] In her book *I Don't Care About Your Band*, the comedian Julie Klausner takes us on a misery tour through the relationships of her twenties, when she tried to decipher the moods of men. OK, maybe she was being naïve for thinking that "when you sleep with somebody after a night of *heavy talking* or pretty much in a scenario where you have the feeling that person might like you . . . you should really be in touch with them the next day." Any fool knows all bets are off when you hook up. But how about when you begin seeing someone regularly? "In a way, even though we'd gone out for a little over a month," she writes about another encounter, "I felt like I knew him and we were close. We spent intimate time together, falling asleep in each other's arms, sharing personal details about ourselves and each other's families. I couldn't imagine how he could be seeing another person on top of that." Reader, he was.[7]

When couples have gotten close enough to move in together, they may still be unsure whether their partners are waving or drowning. They could be "a little bit married," as the writer Hannah Seligson describes it.[8] Or they could be trying to finesse the wicked real estate market. A lot of couples drift into living together because they've been dating for a while, one of them loses a roommate, and why not? Other men and women are making a deliberate statement that they are a Serious Couple, not that this clarifies things. Women are more likely than men to assume that once they are living together, the proposal is coming next, according to research quoted by Seligson. Women are also more inclined to make sacrifices for the sake of the long-term relationship—say, moving to another city or visiting his parents instead of hers at Christmas. Men? Not so much. "For men," writes Pamela Smock, one of the leading researchers in the area, "marriage was not necessarily the goal of cohabitation."[9]

Now, you could argue that preadults are navigating a transitional era when the old conventions of mating are dead and new ones are yet to be born. When they live in groups, humans naturally create some kind of predictable order in their relations, and so will preadults in time. There's something to this idea. The Internet is filled with attempts to provide new rules, everything from "How Should a Woman Like Yourself Dress for a Date" to (ahem) whether to spit or swallow. Here, for instance, is an example, an effort to design the proper "etiquette for a one-night stand."

> Once the fling has been flung, get out. Waking up together is very "couple-y," and curling up next to a warm body can breed attachment. That doesn't mean you need to bolt for the door (or kick him out) as soon as the deed is done. A few minutes of conversation followed by a "Thanks for coming over," or an "I really should get home," sends the message with minimal drama. Sometimes, though, sleep happens. Whether there was enough chemistry to seduce you into basking in the afterglow or whether alcohol made it impossible or impractical to hit the road, you've now got to get out of there in the light of day. Best-case scenario: Both parties are clear in advance that the encounter will only be for one night, and you part ways with a simple, "That was fun. Take care." Unfortunately, the combination of alcohol and hormones may mean that you skipped the first step (clarifying expectations), and you could roll over, open your eyes and say to yourself, "Oh, my God. What did I do?" or worse, "Who the hell is this?"[10]

Though the unpaid one-night stand may be a modern custom, notice that the goal of the advice proffered here is as old as manners themselves: ritualized behavior designed to respect the other person's feelings.

One striking characteristic of the etiquette for a one-night stand is its androgyny. It applies to both men and women. This sets it apart from previous mating conventions designed around presumed differences between the sexes. In the dating era, men did the pursuing and wooing; planning the date, opening doors, and paying for the movie was a demonstration in microcosm of his skills as provider and protector. Women had to show that they were attractive, pleasing, and not too sexually eager; a smart-aleck didn't promise a happy home, and one with a sexual history was a bad bet if you wanted to be sure her children were also yours. But today, women and men meet as equals—socially, professionally, and sexually; no doubt a lot of twentysomething guys think of girls as more together than they are. At the very least, they have had years of experience as equal competitors—in school, on soccer fields, and in bed. While specific etiquette may be ambiguous, men and women can reasonably assume that the people they are meeting at the bar or café or gym are after the same things they are: financial independence, career success, toned triceps, and sex.

Except, despite the general free-for-all and despite the existence of Miss Manners of the one-night stand, preadults have been reluctant to dispense with the old dating gender rules. On the contrary. They are attached to those rules in a way that suggests ambivalence, at the very least, to androgynous courtship. Jillian Strauss, who interviewed one hundred educated, urban singles for her book *Unhooked Generation*, discovered many enlightened women with remarkably traditional "personal scripts," that is, explicit ideas about how a guy should act if he's going to merit a second look. These included walking a woman home or helping her on with her coat. Strauss describes Lisa, a 26-year-old journalist fixed up for a date with a 29-year-old social worker. When he arrives at her door, she's delighted to see that he's as good-looking as advertised. But when they walk to his car, he makes his first mistake: he fails to open the car door for her. Mistake number two comes a moment later: instead of telling her what he had planned for the evening, he asks, "So what would you like to do?" "Her idea of a date is that the man plans the evening and takes the woman out," Strauss explains.[11] Never mind that the Doesn't-Open-the-Car-Door Guy may well have been chewed out by a female colleague for reaching for the office door the previous week.

Maybe Lisa is just a Rules girl, a silly throwback to the Fonzie era. But the ghosts of manhood past linger all throughout the preadult scene, from Washington, DC, preppies to Seattle hipsters. Consider the moment the dinner check arrives. The question of who grabs it is a subject of endless discussion on the hundreds of Internet dating sites. The general consensus among women seems to be that a guy should pay on a first date. Strauss confirms that for her female subjects, if a guy doesn't do that, it's a deal breaker. Men tend to agree: guys pay for dinner. On the popular dating website The Frisky, writer John DeVore has this hoary explanation: "The dude will take care of it because that's what dudes do. There are some things the male of the species will always be in charge of, like bear defense. You know what else? Buying dinner on the first date."[12] Some men even take a woman's insistence at sharing the check as a sign that she isn't interested. Other men assume they should pay for dinner early in the relationship, but if a woman doesn't offer to pick up a check after a decent interval (the third date? the fifth? Does Starbucks count?), it's a bad sign—she thinks she is a princess, and she should be summarily dropped.

But other men find *any* presumption that they should pay galling. If you think about it logically—though by now you may be understandably wondering just how much logic applies in matters of this sort—they have a point. Men and women are supposed to be equal. Women resent other signs of male clout; why not this one? Why, when it comes to money, are women suddenly playing coy? After all, at this stage in their lives a lot of them are earning more than the guys they are dating. Julie Klausner managed to find herself one guy so principled in this regard that he expected to split the check for a dinner he initiated to celebrate her birthday.[13]

The dinner check quandary captures the puzzling predicament of young men in pursuit: they are caught between women's persistent attraction to male vigor, or manhood of an old-fashioned variety, and the vibrator-powered womanhood of today. On the one hand, a woman wants Ashley Wilkes, all sensitivity and soulfulness and attention to "her needs." On the other, she wants Rhett Butler, sultry, confident, and capable of the grand gesture. If on Valentine's Day he gives her a single stem, she may be all "One rose? That's it?" If he wants to get married, he has to plan a proposal on the order of a Hollywood production. The proposal is a particularly odd relic in preadult culture. If men and women are equals, it makes no sense to expect men to propose. Shouldn't a couple make a decision together, as they would about where to go for brunch?

Instead, the young man trying to do the right thing finds himself competing with the likes of Joel Kimmel, who got some Internet attention when he proposed to his girlfriend of five years by writing and illustrating a short story with an antique brass ring with a coral Art Nouveau design hidden on the last page. Another heroic fiancé earned a few minutes of fame by performing a musical in the middle of a city park. The last song of the show ends with him making a declaration of enduring love and planting a ring on the finger of his demurely seated intended. A nice dinner with a ring placed at the bottom of the chocolate mousse? Forget it.

What's a guy to do? He grew up hearing from his mother, his teachers, and Oprah that women wanted "sensitive," "kind," "thoughtful" men who are in touch with their feminine side, who share their feelings, who enjoy watching *Desperate Housewives* rather than *Jackass 3*. Yeah, right, sneer a lot of veterans of the scene. Women really want men with muscles, gumption, and maybe even a whiff of danger. One popular dating guru, David DeAngelo, lists "Being Too Much of a Nice Guy" as number one in his "Ten Most Dangerous Mistakes Men Make With Women." At a website with the evocative name Relationshit.com (sociological cousin of Dating-is-Hell.net), the most highly trafficked pages are those dedicated to the question of why women don't like sweet guys. A book and website called Hotchickswithdouchebags.com rubs it in by offering pictures of jerks—we know by their ripped jeans, five o'clock shadow, gelled hair, and bling—standing next to adoring, bikini-clad blondes.

The lament of nice guys disillusioned by a putative female pref-erence for jerks and assholes has become a common trope in the dating literature. The female complaint has it that "there are no single men. They're all either gay, married, or losers." Sometimes women are kind enough to say this in *front* of single men. "Now I knew lots of available single guys, including myself," one San Francisco single guy wrote angrily in a column on Geocities.com. "So this mantra translated was: 'I can't attract the males I want, therefore I will subtly demean all of them, including you.'"[14] "A Recovering Nice Guy" on the Los Angeles Craigslist had a slightly different take in addressing the question, "What happened to all the nice guys?" His answer is: "You did. You ignored the nice guy. You used him for emotional intimacy without reciprocating, in kind, with physical intimacy." Women, he says, are actually not attracted to men who hold doors open for them or give them a hinted-for Christmas gift or listen to their tales of woe. If the nice guy was smart, our Recovering NG continues, "he came to realize that, if he wanted a woman like you, he'd have to act more like the boyfriend that you had. He probably cleaned up his look, started making some money, and generally acted like more of an asshole than he ever wanted to be."[15]

The disenchanted young man may conclude: no more Mr. Nice Guy! He will stand up for manly men, and in the process, give women what they actually want, rather than what they pretend they want. He will put those lessons he got all throughout his over-feminized childhood and adolescence in the shredder and join what the *Boston Globe* has called "the Menaissance."[16] Menaissance men celebrate the revival of macho in books with such titles as *The Alphabet of Manliness* (example: K is for Knockers, Q is for Quickies), *The Retrosexual Manual, Being the Strong Man a Woman Wants,* or the recent *Real Men Don't Apologize,* by actor Jim Belushi.

Charles Darwin is the guiding philosopher of the Menaissance Man. The theory that human sexual preferences evolved from the time that bipedal hominids successfully reproduced in the primeval African grasslands can supposedly explain the mystery of women's preference for macho—or alpha—males. That's when females reached the conclusion that their best bet for the survival of their future children was a dominant male. Applicable in a Chicago bar or not, the theory gives the former wuss permission to loudly proclaim his urge to have massive amounts of sex with an endless assortment of women and to otherwise puff out his chest. Culture, in both its feminist and Emily Post forms, hasn't won him any favor with women, so he will embrace nature no matter how incorrect it seems. Yes, he concludes, it's a savannah out there; best to adapt to its exigencies.

For a good illustration of the Darwinian approach to dating etiquette, consider what's known as the Seduction Community. The Community is a loose network of dating coaches and gurus and their followers whose philosophical origins lie variously in Darwin, Norman Vincent Peale, and hyper-logical geekdom. Women don't want child-men or nice guys, goes their theory. They want alpha males, and with some effort at self-improvement, any man can learn the game—Game, as it is reverently known—that will turn him into an alpha, or a Pick-Up Artist (PUA). A highly skilled PUA can get any woman, even an HB10 (Hot Babe who is a perfect 10; Game has more acronyms and rankings than the DOD). It's impossible to know just how many wannabe PUAs there are out there, but judging from the multitude of websites, such as Alpha Man Seduction, FastSeduction, StreetSmartDating, GrowYourGame, SeductionTutor, and SeductionChronicles; ads for seduction gurus, chat rooms, conferences, and boot camps not just in the United States but all over Europe and parts of Asia; and books, including Neil Strauss's 2005 best seller titled *The Game*, their numbers are considerable.

Rejecting all manners that enshrined respect and care in an area of human interaction rife with opportunities for pain and humiliation, dating Darwinists unapologetically endorse ruthlessness and deception. "You see, Nature doesn't care about hurting people's feelings," explains dating coach Mike Pilinski, also author of *Without Embarrassment: The Social Coward's Totally Fearless Seduction System*. "It cares ONLY about reproductive success in order to keep those precious DNA molecules traveling forward in Time."[17] Game, for instance, encourages men to "neg" their "target" woman, that is, to subtly undermine her confidence by ignoring or mildly insulting her ("Huh. I just saw another woman wearing that dress."). The hotter the woman, the more essential it is to neg her because attractive women with higher self-esteem are harder to keep off-balance.

Game is best understood as a male attempt to bring order to contemporary dating disarray and a child-man's effort to relearn the primal masculinity he had been taught to suppress. "Things don't make sense anymore, that's why we need pickup," as one commenter on FastSeduction.com put it. That goal means desensitizing men, relieving them of the very feelings they were taught women wanted them to express. Teachers encourage clients to project confidence and sexual energy, what is called, depending on the guru, "cocky funny" or "amused mastery." A writer named Kevin Purcell writes of his experience at a Game workshop in *The Aquarian,* a music magazine based in New York: "One of our first tasks was to walk around the hotel silent, repeating in our heads 'I don't give a fuck what anyone thinks about me.' This mentality, it was assumed, would help lower the wall of anxiety and make us less prone to the pain of rejection. Like soldiers responding to a drill sergeant, when asked, 'What are you?' we were instructed to loudly proclaim, 'A fucking ten!'"[18]

You have to hand the Game theorists this much: Darwinian mores—or anti-mores—help explain the high-stakes status-jockeying that pervades the contemporary dating scene. Check out Darwindating.com, a matchmaking website "created exclusively for beautiful, desirable people." Members rank your picture on a scale of 1 to 5 and vote whether to let you join their honored ranks or throw you into the slush pile of "saggy," "hairy," "sweaty," "nerdy" rejects. My 29-year-old daughter told me of a friend, a Yale and Stanford business school graduate, who asked her apropos of nothing: "If you rank women from 1 to 10, 1 being Ugly Betty and 10 being Elizabeth Hurley, what number could I get?" Jillian Strauss describes a 34-year-old sales manager from Dallas who says his current girlfriend meets only six out of his ten requirements for the perfect girlfriend. When they go out together, he is constantly looking out for an "upgrade."[19]

Crude, callow, and just all-around despicable? Of course. But men are convinced that they are no worse—and probably a good deal better—than women in making these calculations, though, with impeccable Darwinian logic, they believe women tend to do their reckoning on the basis of wallet size rather than pulchritude. Hypergamy is the expert term for the female urge to mate up in the status hierarchy. What it adds up to is that neither sex can be trusted. Men cheat because they are always hunting for variety, while women double-deal because they are always prowling for higher-status males. "Attractive single girls not only dropped their 'dates' at the slightest whiff of a bigger, better deal, they routinely betrayed their girlfriends, too," Toby Young, a British author who lived in New York for five years, wrote about his sojourn there in his dismissive review of the movie *Sex and the City*.[20]

Actually, though it wasn't duly appreciated for it, and though the subject was treated far more pointedly in Candace Bushnell's original book on which the series was based, *Sex and the City* provided a brilliantly biting commentary on hypergamy or, more generally, the status game in the urban dating environment. The four alpha girl characters struggle to find a mate worthy of their knowledge economy status. The series' writers grasped how much status in that economy is based not on money (or not exclusively on money) but on impressive education credentials and cool jobs. The first thing we learn about almost every new character is his profession, and the list could make up a social registry of the knowledge economy: "a broker who made two million on bonds last year"; a litigator "who takes steam baths with Ronald Perelman"; a Harvard MBA; a publishing magnate; an architect; a documentary filmmaker; a composer of movie music; an actor; a labor lawyer; a divorce lawyer; a dermatologist; an ophthalmologist; an orthopedic surgeon; an internist; and, of course, the most creative of the brainy elite, "an editor at a hip political magazine," a writer for *The Economist,* and a "short story writer."

Played by the endearing Sarah Jessica Parker, Carrie Bradshaw appears generous and warm, but if you scratch the surface—sorry, SJP fans—she is the most cold-blooded of these alpha male huntresses. Miranda the Harvard-educated lawyer, after all, marries Steve. He may be a nobody, but he is a down-to-earth, generous nobody who loves her and is the father of her baby. On the other hand, when Carrie falls for Aidan, whom she calls "the perfect boyfriend," a furniture maker and a man who not only knows how to use tools but who loves sports, beer, and Kentucky Fried Chicken, it's clear the relationship is doomed. Aidan's habits make him seem like a guy from the outer boroughs or worse, a loser . . . from New Jersey. ("I don't do boroughs," Carrie's friend Samantha, the most outspoken of these snobs, sniffs when one of her boy toys asks her to come see him in a theater production in Brooklyn.) As his only half-facetious name suggests, Carrie's true love, Mr. Big, is pure alpha—rich, smooth, and, as if proving the conclusions of recovering nice guys everywhere, a bit of a jerk. No doubt about it: Big's wealth is at the heart of his masculine appeal. He travels in a limousine in expensive suits and immaculately pressed white shirts. ("Cabs are bullshit," he grumbles when he is forced to travel in one with Carrie and a jazz musician they met at a downtown club.) But his confidence and dominance are also a big part of his appeal. Big understands Carrie's weak spot when it comes to Aidan's status. Calling him Paul Bunyan and Daniel Boone, he sneers: "I can smell the guy on your sheets. Wood chips and Paco Rabane," referring to a cheap men's cologne. In the higher reaches of the knowledge economy, real men wear Gucci.

Are the dating Darwinists, who evidently include the creators of *Sex and the City,* right? Do women always prefer rich alpha males? That's putting it far too crudely. Money isn't everything; especially in a technology-, media-, and design-rich economy, intelligence, creativity, and charismatic people skills can bring significant prestige to their owners and the women with whom they consort. A lot of women who are earning good money might trade high income in a mate for the cachet a clever painter or writer brings to the dinner party table. There's some survey evidence that when women have their own sources of wealth—as women with high IQs and college degrees have in a knowledge economy—they are less concerned about a man's wallet. Examining the mate preferences of college students since 1939, the sociologist Christine Whalen found a decrease in the percentage of women who rank money high on their list. Today, only a small percentage of high-achieving women say they are set on finding a man more educated than they are, and slightly more say they want more "accomplished" men.[21] In fact, more than one-third of the high-rolling women say they would prefer to marry someone more easygoing than they are.[22] They appear to mean business because as of 2007, about 22 percent of married women were earning more than their husbands, compared with 4 percent in 1970.[23]

Still, the Darwinians have the preponderance of evidence in their corner: forty years after they threw off the feminine mystique, most women continue to prefer bigger, stronger, richer men—at least as husbands—just as they have in every culture.[24] They typically marry men who are taller than they are, men who are several years older than they are (though the age difference has declined in recent decades in the United States), and men who earn more than they do (though that number, too, has declined a bit). Data from dating websites provide a wealth of information about the preferences of both men and women, and they almost always support the Darwinians. One soon-to-be-published study, for instance, found that while both sexes are looking for attractive partners, women are considerably more likely to contact men with higher income and education than vice versa.[25] Everyone knows the woman who calls herself a feminist but still wants "a guy to be a guy" or who says something along the lines of "I didn't need a guy to take care of me, but I wouldn't be with someone who couldn't." Such women want the option of a few years at home with the children, though they are deeply offended if a guy says he wants a wife who will do exactly that.[26] The cynics have a point, don't they?

Darwin haunts the dating scene in another respect. Even though we often hear that millennials are a postracial generation, white customers of dating websites, especially women, prefer to date white men.[27] Could it be that white men equal success in women's minds? Some researchers say that Asian men are the lowest men on the dating totem pole, a fact that those men have figured out from firsthand experience. Bitterasianmen.com is a chat room for, well, bitter Asian men who are convinced "white girls don't want us." As they themselves have noted, Darwinians have the only compelling explanation for this; Asian men tend to be smaller and shyer (i.e., less dominant) than men of other races.[28]

The Hollywood dream factory pays its respects to Darwin, producing a steady pageant of proverbial man's men for women to ogle and men to admire. Which they do—by the millions. Think of today's popular heartthrobs, such as Matt Damon, Ben Affleck, and Brad Pitt; all of them have the shoulders, biceps, and abs of Marines. Ed Bernero, a Hollywood producer, argues that the popularity of the television series *Two and a Half Men* is because of women's attraction to the adorable bad boy Charlie Sheen. They are convinced this wild man can be tamed by the right woman, meaning, in their dream life, themselves.[29] Why do women swoon—and yes, that seems the right word—over Jon Hamm's portrayal of Don Draper in *Mad Men*? They love the cool swagger of a dominant male.[30] We might also nod at Tucker Max, the bad boy we met in Chapter 5. If Max is telling the truth only a fraction of the time—and there's reason to think he's on target more than that[31]—then sexual strutting even in the most obnoxious man attracts women by the busload.

Aside from the knowledge economy status struggle, there is another, even more insidious influence on the Darwinian tenor of the current mating regime: the later age of marriage. Most people know the story by now. Women are at their most fertile in their mid-twenties. By 30, their fertility begins to decline; after 35, the decline picks up the pace. By 40, one in five women is infertile; those who do get pregnant are more prone to miscarriage and genetic abnormalities.[32] The impact of these hard biological realities on preadult romantic lives is profound, more so than most twentysomethings can grasp. When a 23-year-old woman is looking for some male attention, she has overflowing shelves to inspect: men from their early twenties to their late thirties or even older. She is not only at her most fertile, she looks her best (a fact that Darwinians would say is no coincidence because smooth, lustrous skin, firm breasts, and a flat belly are nature's way of signaling health, youth, and fertility). By 30, that same woman is looking at a much smaller larder of men. Meanwhile, men in their thirties—her peers—now have an ever-growing selection of young women to choose from.

These truths understandably make young women want to scream; they seem like an invention dreamed up by Dr. Misogyny to defraud them of the freedom they were promised during their girl-powered childhoods. Some try to put the blame on a Megan Fox–obsessed media or more generally on culturally perpetuated sexism. Even if they were right about the causes—something that seems unlikely given that the male preference for younger females exists in every culture under the sun—the fact remains that men are far less likely to find older women appealing than vice versa. The number-crunchers at the dating website OK Cupid have discovered that as they age, women get fewer and fewer messages from prospective dates; the same cleavage shots that brought in a lot of interested guys in their twenties are duds when women post them in their thirties. The median 31-year-old guy says in his post that he is interested in women between 22 and 35—nine years younger, but only four years older, than himself. This skewed mind-set worsens with age; the median 42-year-old will accept a woman up to fifteen years younger, but no more than three years older. If anything, men are in denial about the extent of their attraction to younger women; they tend to pursue the youngest dates in their stated range or go after those even younger than that.[33]

Preadult women and men, then, are on opposite trajectories. Once they get past the awkward years—the late teens and early twenties—men begin to lose their metaphorical baby fat. They're making more money, the pool of available women is growing, and they have more confidence. "I could get a woman now, but when I'm 30 or 35 I could do better," Bryson Turner, a thoughtful 24-year-old from Washington, DC, told me in an interview, before adding with a sheepish laugh, "Women really don't have a choice. We called them on their bluff."[34] Bryson is right; women live his life in reverse. In their early twenties, they are a hot commodity; by their early thirties, their luster is dimming. "A woman's biggest enemy is time," explains one popular web observer of the contemporary dating environment. "When a woman graduates from college at the age of 22, she thinks she has all the time in the world. She builds up her social circle to prepare for *years* of drinking and partying. . . . Then 28 and 29 passes and all she has to show for the previous near-decade is a cell phone filled with numbers of guys she 'dated.' She hits day spas, gets botox, and then cruises the internet and clubs with a renewed vigor. But it doesn't work, and 35 is here before you know it."[35]

Laura Nolan, the single and demoralized thirtysomething woman writing in the *Times of London* whom we met in the Introduction, theorizes that the men she knows, instead of having their flings and then settling down, actually grow *more* skittish about relationships as they move from their twenties to thirties: "The [younger man] who fell in love and believed that when you found a great girl you counted your blessings and married her has morphed into someone in search of nothing more than a bit of fun, who views any relationship that he can't get out of at the ping of a text message with genuine unease."[36] A reaction to Nolan's article from one man, entitled "Revenge of the Geek," is worth quoting at length because it so perfectly captures one common mind-set of the single thirtysomething child-man:

> Here is a population of ordinary guys—the guys who were nothing special, the dorks who were passed over in favour of the cool, attractive guys when they were younger. And now, possibly for the first time in history, they find themselves in an unreal bubble. Women are no longer being cautious and picky—they are competing for their attentions. This is a genuine turning point in the history of gender relations. For the first time ever, geeks and bozos have pulling power. Can you blame them, after thousands of years of competing for female attention, for letting it go to their heads?

And then I thought: hang on a minute. I was one of those geeks. As I got older and less physically attractive, I found it easier and easier to talk to women. This was weird. Was it not supposed to happen the other way around? I was overweight. I had a drinking problem. But women, who had seemed elusive in my teens and early twenties, were always there for me, even if I wasn't always there for them. For years, I did not commit. Even worse than that—for years, I half-committed, in one relationship after another. I wasted years of people's time. . . .

Women in their thirties feel aggrieved that men in their thirties won't commit to them. But aren't these thirtysomething women the very same people who snagged the slightly older men ten years before?[37]

What all of this adds up to for women is a gap between the cultural ideals behind preadulthood—equality, freedom, personal achievement, sexual self-expression—and biology's pitiless clock. It's a gap that over the long run works to their disadvantage, and it lies at the heart of many contemporary women's complaints. The "Women's Interest" shelf is crowded with the tales of successful late-thirty- and fortysomething women either puzzling over the lonely middle age looming before them or proclaiming their determination to live a good life on their own. "Thirtysomethings might notice that there are generally fewer parties to go to, since our friends are otherwise engaged with their babies—or even just with being engaged," writes one participant/observer. "And when you do go to a party, the male guests are unavailable. Like, all of the male guests. Ah, dating in your thirties. Do your best to find someone before you get here."[38] The most notorious example of the single thirtysomething lament is Lori Gottlieb's book *Marry Him: The Case for Settling for Mr. Good Enough*. In her late thirties with no husband on the horizon, Gottlieb bought some sperm and had herself a son. At 40, still longing for a man to complete her family, she questions whether she had been too picky in her youth. "It seemed reasonable that the longer I searched, the better the guy I'd end up with."[39] Reasonable on Pandora, maybe, but not here on Earth, where two sexes mean two divergent calendars. Gottlieb got plenty of push-back, some of it justifiable, from scribbling women who objected to her broad portrayal of the single woman's plight. One thing her critics could not dispute, however, was the grim Darwinian logic of aging and mating that lay behind Gottlieb's predicament and that of others in the surprised single sisterhood.

Men sense the increasing desperation of the thirtysomething woman; this adds to their advantage—and their cynicism. Even nice guys might resent the feeling that, say, a 34-year-old single magazine editor sees herself as "settling" and is less interested in him than in what he represents: a sperm-and-child-support delivery system. Your average less-than-nice guy, taking note of the power differential between himself and his prospective dates, can get just plain nasty. Jenny Blake, a popular blogger on quarterlife issues, describes being in a "dating desert." "I've been on exactly two second dates in a year and a half during one of which the guy told me, 'Women are like cars—better to lease then trade up when you're done.'"[40] "We can be slovenly from the start," one interview subject told Amy Cohen in her now-defunct dating column for the *New York Observer*, "because we can get laid anytime we want."[41] Remember those women who think a man ought to open the car door for them? They'll be lucky if the find a guy willing to add "please" to "pass the ketchup." Women complain that instead of calling to ask them out, or even make plans for a date, men simply text, "Heading downtown. Where r u?" as they walk

to the subway station or get in their car. Manners, some have figured, are optional when you have most of the power and Emily
Post is long dead. "There is no longer any reason to answer the
phone when a woman calls you or return her call when she leaves
you a message," insists one dating pro on the Quarterlife blog.
"What should you do? Text message, of course."

Does the Darwinian lens shed an overly harsh light on the present generation of men—and women? Not really. They're just human. Their problem is coming of age in a culture without reliable
conventions to tame the raw egotism and roughness of nature's
mating dance. It's all about sex anyway, a lot of guys conclude, so
why dress it all up in silly manners? Jillian Strauss recalls meeting a
man at a Hamptons pool party who early on in their conversation
asked: "So, are you getting any?"[42] One of Amy Cohen's lessons in
contemporary politesse came on a first date with a man who asked
her how many guys she had slept with and whether she owned a
vibrator.[43] Here's a collection of dating "don'ts" from several young
feminist websites, all of them a reflection of bitter experience:
"Don't tell me on a first date about the time you were tested for
chlamydia (because you found out your high school girlfriend was 'a
bit of a skank') and go on to describe in loving detail the sensation
of a medical-grade Q-tip being inserted into your penis."[44] "Don't
pull the feminist card on me when I won't hook up with you. 'You
know Jill, there was this little thing called the Sexual Revolution . . .' is not a particularly good strategy. Neither is asking me
how much money you have to spend before sex is on the table."[45]
"Don't pre-emptively tell me you have a small penis." "Don't text
me on a Tuesday night after midnight 'I could totally eat ur puss
now if u r interwssetted.' I'm not."[46]

To be fair, women are not in a good position to complain.
They have been known to sext pictures of their naked lady parts

to men they barely know, to groan, "I need to get laid" in mixed company, and to wear T-shirts promising "My Boyfriend's Out of Town." When the singer Jessica Simpson was photographed wearing a T-shirt saying "Real Girls Eat Meat," People for the Ethical Treatment of Animals objected, but that was about it. At a forum on Quarterlife.com, a website for twentysomethings, a female poster describes a digital flirtation with a guy who sends her a picture of his penis, or as she puts it, his "junk." In the current mating environment, immature assholery alone cannot explain guys who assume women will take a picture of their "junk" in stride.

The most surprising thing about the current dating and mating scene is that most men and women seem to grow out of it. For a number of decades now, men and women with college degrees have married at greater rates and with more success than those without. The question that inescapably presents itself is this: with untamed Darwinism ascendant, can that possibly last?

seven

MANNING UP?

What should I do with my life? Inevitably, though not necessarily mindfully, the question will find an answer. Time passes and the preadult becomes a decided adult, slouching toward middle age and reading glasses. Preadults won't have much trouble taking their places in what we called in the 1960s "the establishment." With the arrival of a complex knowledge economy, there are enough interesting ways to make a living to satisfy most of them, and women especially seem ready and eager to become the bosses, business owners, executives, legislators, managers, board members, professors, and partners of tomorrow.

Whether America's future professional/ruling class will be similarly eager and competent on the home front is another question. Like all previous generations, millennials are only here for a brief visit; they will need to create the families and raise the children to take their place when they are gone. Given the general chaos and ambiguity of the mating scene, how will that happen? Will men and women be able to raise the next generation together? Will men man up? Will women have them? Let's look at a few common scenarios of what's happening right now:

SCENARIO 1: The Neo-Traditional. They met when they were both students at Wesleyan. They flirted briefly, but they were both involved with other people, and nothing came of it. After graduation, he spent a year in China teaching English, then went to business school at NYU, and then to an executive position at McCann Erikson. He had a number of relationships; one was pretty serious, but it ended when she moved to study animation at Cal Arts. She worked for a year as a paralegal, went to NYU Law, and took a job in the estates division at Sullivan Cromwell. They reconnected at a party of Wesleyan friends, and over the next year they became inseparable, including holidays that they carefully distributed between their families. The night they moved in together, he proposed by putting his late grandmother's diamond ring, a bottle of Veuve-Cliquot, and two carefully wrapped Baccarat crystal flutes in the bottom of the box containing her old tennis trophies. She cried and said yes. A year and a half later they were married at a Sonoma winery. He was 30 and she was 29, just about average for their demographic, and other than disappointment over the fact that their story would not appear in the *New York Times* Vows section—it struck the editor as unexceptional—the couple and their families were over the moon.

Safe prediction: they will go through some bad times, particularly when their two children are young—marital happiness declines when the kids come along and ruin the rhythm of independent life (sex, sleep, movies, dinner)[1]—but they will stay together even as the kids graduate from Wesleyan and start their own preadult lives.

SCENARIO 2: The Darwinian Playboy. These are the guys who plan to live alone and have a lot of sex with a lot of women. Though they might hang around for a while, they will never, ever be that into you. They lard their deep mistrust of women with convenient bits of evolutionary psychology. Some saw fathers, uncles, brothers, or friends chewed up and spit out by ex-wives who had cheated on them but still got the house, the kids, and half their ex's income. Others probably never recovered from their own experience of betrayal; others are geeks who, having spent much of their twenties invisible to women, are also in a vengeful frame of mind. Some of them are devoted followers of Roissy, a philosophically sophisticated blogger who uses his multitudinous sexual encounters to analyze the amoral nature of female desire; think Hefner via Dostoyevsky. Women, no matter how determinedly enlightened and independent, are turned on by smart, dominant males—not bullies, not necessarily billionaires, mind you, but guys who know how to communicate the right mix of self-confidence, aloofness, and charisma. Love and marriage, concludes Roissy, are just "pretty lies." "Marriage is no escape from the sexual market and the possibility that you may be outbid by a competitor with higher value," he writes. "No matter how much you love your kids, if a divorce happens (50% chance, 70+% chance the wife initiates it) you are going to be paying child support for the new lingerie your ex-wife buys to sexually please her blogger lover. Life is a parade of worry and high wire risk, of love and loneliness, and no socially manufactured arrangement exists to insulate you from your dreaded fears. To imagine otherwise is beta."[2]

Safe prediction: By his mid-forties, the Playboy is doing a comb-over for his balding head and wearing leather jackets to cover up his gut when he goes to bars to pick up women. Despite the fact that he tends to blather on about great bands of the 1990s, there are a few who are willing to sleep with him. Eventually, he'll find himself seeing one of them and deciding to move in with her. He becomes a stepdad to her kids and begins to dislike her ex as much as she does. He's not especially happy with his arrangement—he remembers the good old days when women appeared to him like an enormous, all-you-can-eat buffet—but now what's the alternative?

SCENARIO 3: The Single-and-Loving-It Woman. These are women who either never wanted to marry or who, in a mirror image of the Darwinian Playboy, dated for years, possibly even got married and then divorced, but in either case concluded they were better off as self-contained units. They are not—repeat, not—waiting for Mr. Right. With interesting jobs and friends, frequent enough dates, occasional relationships, and exciting trips and hobbies, they bristle at the old idea that a female singleton is a woman manqué. They might approvingly quote the (unmarried) actress Renée Zellweger: "I'm not single, I'm busy." Most single-and-loving-it women are content with their lives and wish would-be matchmakers and pitiers would calm down. But some, such as Bella DePaulo, the Rosa Luxemburg of the demographic, have taken their status on as a moral crusade. A Harvard-trained social psychologist, author of *Singled Out: How Singles Are Stereotyped, Stigmatized and Ignored and Still Live Happily Ever After*, and author of the "Living Single" column for *Psychology Today*, DePaulo has introduced the term "singlism." Like racists and sexists, singlists discriminate against an outcast group. In her column, which makes up in passion what it lacks in scientific rigor, DePaulo enumerates the many slights against singles and insists that despite their bad rap as isolated and selfish, they are actually more helpful to parents, siblings, friends, and neighbors than smug "marrieds," in Bridget Jones's words.[3]

Safe-ish prediction: the single-and-loving-it woman will have satisfying work; a lot of travel, concerts, lectures, friends, and close relationships with nieces and nephews who will try not to resent it when they are called on to help when she needs a hip replacement in her fifties. She will have occasional lovers, one or two of them even treating her to mind-blowing sex, but gradually the opportunities will dwindle to once every few years. That's if she's lucky. The sex ratio drops steadily by age and the chances of finding any man—not to mention a sexually functioning man—without an already packed dance card dwindles to almost nothing.[4] (See writer Amy Cohen's description of watching along with her single thirtysomething friends as her newly widowed father attracts women like he's Mick Jagger.)[5]

SCENARIO 4: The Choice Mother. At first, Rachel Lehman-Haupt comes across as the enviable heroine in a chick-lit film. "When I'm not writing at my desk in the West Village," she writes on her website, "I'm somewhere in the world on assignment—I've gone undercover with prostitutes and ravers, observed fashion trends in American malls, explored (and sometimes surfed) secret beaches, and worked on stories in India, South Africa, Italy and Argentina as well as in the backyard of Manhattan and at my favorite coffee shop, MoJo, around the corner from my home." Unlike Carrie Bradshaw—though like most women—she was hoping for a husband and a baby to complete the picture. When she was in her early twenties, she fell for and lived happily with a guy named Andrew. But as she describes it in her 2009 memoir *In Her Own Sweet Time*, she "fell in love with journalism" instead. Her growing ambitions made Andrew, who was a lively, outdoorsy kind of guy but no Mr. Big, seem subpar. She left him, had many dates and relationships, but still found no husband. "And so here I am, almost eight years after my breakup with Andrew. I'm on firmer ground in my identity and career, and I'm free to go anywhere I want," Lehman-Haupt writes at the beginning of her book about the irony of her situation. "But now, just shy of my thirty-fifth birthday, this is where I've chosen to go: a fertility clinic."[6] At the fertility clinic, she begins a research process that leads her to freeze her eggs in hopes that either she will eventually be able to use them with a man she wants to marry, or, failing that, pay a sperm donor so that she can raise a child on her own. Meanwhile, she wonders whether she made some bad decisions (e.g., dumping Andrew) along the way to adulthood.

Safe prediction: The Choice Mother is something new under the sun. There is no safe prediction.

SCENARIO 5: The Starter Marriage. Sascha Rothchild is a fine example of this scenario. The author of "How To Get Divorced by 30," she dated her husband, Dan, a child-man if there ever was one, for three years. He was a video-gaming stoner, passive about his future, but attached to his Type A girlfriend. His idea of a proposal was rolling over in bed one morning and saying, "So, how do you want to do this?" As for Rothchild, she had wanted to marry because she was bent on following an "arbitrary time-table"; at any rate, "marriage at the time seemed easier than breaking up." They had a "cool" wedding, which meant avoiding words like "love" and "forever." All of this may or may not have been influenced by the fact that both of her parents had been divorced in their twenties.

By the time she turned 30, she wanted out, which turned out to be an excellent career move. While she was on her book tour, her next boyfriend planned "a proposal fit for a big budget studio romantic comedy"; it would be filmed at the top of a mountain sunset by the Snowcat driver. As of April 2010, she was engaged once again. She knows that second marriages have an even worse record than first marriages, but she says that's because most people going into a second marriage don't ask themselves what they did wrong the first time around. This one will work out, she knows, because she and her intended go out and do fun things together, they make a lot of compromises like going to Cubs games for him and shopping for shoes for her—and like all successfully married couples, they've planned to use the word "love," buy an expensive dress, *and* hire a wedding planner for their nuptials.[7]

Safe prediction: I wouldn't dare.

The good news is that the first scenario—a decade or so of dating and relationships, culminating in the wedding and kids—is by far the most common. I say "good news" for two reasons. First, that's what most people want. If you've been reading some media stories, you may be under a different impression. It's commonly reported that marriage is dead, an archaic institution with little relevance for today. In northwest Europe and Canada, this belief has a substantial number of takers, though even there, it remains a minority view.[8]

But in the United States, marriage is still devoutly wished for by every class of people, including the college educated. Not so long ago, educated women were generally thought of as a spinster class—men didn't want to marry brainy women. Today's college-educated woman is a new figure entirely. She is as likely to become wife and mother as less-educated women. According to a study by a University of Pennsylvania economist, in the United States in 2008, 86 percent of college-educated white women were married by age 40, compared with 88 percent of those with less than a four-year degree. The numbers for white, college-educated men are similar: 84 percent of them were married by 40 in 2008. The conventional wisdom, not borne out by research, by the way, may have it that marriage is a raw deal for women. But college-educated white women don't seem to believe it. They are the most likely of any group to think that "married people are generally happier than unmarried people."[9] When you ask high school seniors, 80 percent or more say they expect—and want—to marry someday, though they're often less than optimistic about their chances of staying married for life.[10] Most people, especially women, think they will be married by their early thirties.[11] The large majority—70 percent—of first-year college students think raising a family is "essential" or "very important" to their futures.[12]

Remember Tucker Max, the author of *I Hope They Serve Beer in Hell* and consummate hook-up artist we met in Chapter 4? A student from Penn State graciously offered to share her experience of having sex with Max after meeting him at a bar near her school. ("I have two options," she writes in her web post "I Slept with Tucker Max" about her decision to become one of Max's ever-growing harem. "One: dignity. Two: a good story to tell later." She chose the second.) During the postcoital pillow talk, Max grew pensive and told her of his "wish to eventually get married and have kids."[13] Ah hah! Even Tucker Max, in the dispiriting event that he can convince some woman he would make a good husband, believes that by 35, "when you should make your major life decisions," he will be stocking the pantry with paper towels, buying roses on his wedding anniversary, and hauling the baby out of the Subaru car seat. If he says so.

The other reason Scenario Number 1's popularity is good news has less to do with the fact that individual men and women like Tucker Max or Rachel Lehman-Haupt want to marry and have kids than with the general social good. After studying the past decades of marital breakdown, social scientists are as sure as it's possible to be in these matters that, assuming the home is abuse-free, children are better off growing up with their married mothers and fathers. At this point in these sorts of discussions, it becomes obligatory to mention how many single mothers are doing a great job and to cite such brilliant, successful children of single mothers as Michael Phelps, Supreme Court justice Sonia Sotomayor, and Barack Obama. These caveats ought to be unnecessary, but Americans seem to have trouble grasping that individual choice—even carefully weighed, rational, intelligent choice—and social goods can be in conflict. No matter how superb the outcome in an individual case, the truth remains that kids growing up in single-parent homes—just about always single-mother homes—are at higher risk of school failure, emotional problems, drug and alcohol abuse, and becoming single parents themselves. When we're talking about an increase in single-parent homes by a magnitude of tens of millions, as has occurred over the past decades, the social and economic costs become immense.

From that vantage point, had it been engineered by a planner in an office of Health and Human Services, preadulthood could be considered a policy success of epic proportions. College-educated mothers are far less likely to divorce than their less educated counterparts. (Whether because of divorce or out-of-wedlock childbearing, a much higher percentage of black children grow up in single-parent homes at every income level.) The reason is pretty clear: people who marry later divorce less. Couples who wait until they are 25 to tie the knot double their chances of staying married.[14] Though the greatest benefits appear by age 25, some research suggests marital stability—though interestingly enough, not marital happiness—continues to improve with every increase in the age of marriage into the late thirties.[15]

Also improving things for the future children of preadults, should trends continue, is that so few of them will be born to single mothers. The vast majority of unmarried new mothers are women in their twenties with a high school degree and some community college. Never-married mothers with a four-year degree are pretty rare (though becoming less so, as we'll see shortly) probably because they know that two hands are better than one in the long, heavy knowledge economy slog—with its little leagues and museum art classes for 4-year-olds, homework hectoring, and the like. They also know from their own experience—the divorce rate among their college-educated boomer mothers was already going down by 1980—that children generally like to have their dads around and keep to their routines.

But whatever their upsides, the truth is that later marriage and childbearing are in an uneasy standoff with human biology, culminating in an unintended set of medical, economic, and social consequences, including more child-men, single mothers, and fatherless homes. As we saw in the previous chapter, women's fertility begins to drop appreciably at 35 (once again, this is an average; many women get pregnant in their forties without difficulty). Between 1990 and 2008, the rate of births among women in older age groups grew exponentially; the number of babies born to women over 35 increased by 64 percent, compared with a growth of just 2 percent among younger women.[16] Problem is, children born to older mothers are at greater risk of autism (older fathers may also contribute to the problem, though their risk has been harder to define).[17] Scientists are also now beginning to discover side effects to assisted reproduction. It's been clear for some time that both later age of childbearing and in vitro fertilization (IVF) produce more multiple births, meaning a greater incidence of low birth weight and all of its associated problems. Now other dangers are coming into view. A recent study of 15,000 French births between 2003 and 2007 found a heightened risk of heart disease and malformation of the urogenital system in boys born through IVF. Another study, published in *Pediatrics*, reports higher rates of childhood cancer among IVF babies.[18] The affected children are still very few—4.24 percent of children, as compared with 2 to 3 percent of children in the French study—but as IVF grows more common, those numbers could begin to have a noticeable social and economic impact.[19]

Moreover, later marriage and childbearing leads to lower birthrates. This will strike many people as another reason to celebrate preadulthood: fewer people mean fewer carbon footprints and environmental relief. It also means demographic disequilibrium. Twenty-seven percent of college-educated women are childless at age 40, and those who have given birth are averaging 1.6 children, substantially lower than the 2.6 rate among the less educated. Harvard sociologists David Ellwood and Christopher Jencks argue that this will have significant economic effects in the future, as companies face a shortage of highly skilled workers and lower productivity.[20] Barely replacement birthrates, such as we have among American women as a whole, also mean an aging population, which tends to mean less innovation and investment down the line. At any rate, someone will have to pay for the medical and basic care for that disproportionate number of older people—and that someone will be this generation of preadults and their children.[21]

The other reason to hold off cheering the arrival of preadulthood can be summed up by Scenarios 2 through 5. Preadulthood represents a historically unique hiatus from family living, and despite the fact that humans have always gravitated toward that arrangement, people can get used to being alone. Over time, women and men come to view potential partners as intruders into their carefully designed single lives. Both the evo-psycho Playboy and the Single and Loving It woman are new cultural types above all because they affirm single living as a uniquely pleasurable lifestyle.

How much that affirmation is a consequence of hard knocks in the dating world is hard to tell, but there is no question that a large number of people in their thirties and forties, after a decade or more of break-ups and broken hearts, are suffering from relationship PTSD. This is hardly the most fertile ground for the future happiness with the opposite sex that most people say they want. The positive spin on waiting to marry has it that you sow your youthful oats, you learn about yourself and what you want, and then you make a good decision about whom to settle down with. It seems to work that way for a lot of people. By no means is it true for everyone. "The idea is that dating should lead toward mating, and spread out before us is this array of choices that *should* lead toward a choice you can feel secure in," the novelist Benjamin Kunkel observed in an interview. "But I think the opposite happens. You become familiar with disposable relationships."[22] Dispose of enough relationships, and you begin to view your exes, whether boyfriends or, in the case of starter marriages, husbands, less as people than as cameo characters in your life story. They are stops on your journey, instruments for your self-awareness. Preadults love to give fictional names to their lovers, like these listed in an article on the relationships website Lemondrop: B.O. Hands, The Sharpie Marker (referring to the size of the penis of the man in question), The Pooper, Skeletor,[23] or the famous moniker The Big Creep, created by one of the first famous preadults, Monica Lewinsky. According to Amy Cohen, when a friend uses the actual name of someone she's dating, saying for instance, "I went out with Mike," it's a sign that a guy may be earning the right to exist outside her storytelling imagination.[24]

Technology, especially dating websites, has also intensified mistrust and defensiveness. If young men and women try to find romantic potential online—a near necessity once dating on campus, crowded with people of the opposite sex the right age and background, gives way to prowling the anonymous city—they find out quickly that everybody lies. At the very least, men add an inch or two to their height; women take away a few pounds.[25] He—or she—never looks like his or her picture. Photoshopping, both literal and figurative, is de rigueur, and manners that might protect other people's feelings completely expendable. "In the fast-paced world of online dating, there is no onus on anyone to be gracious, kind, or even honest—or to give anyone a second chance," Lehman-Haupt observes.[26] One guy contacts her, but he wants to see a picture of her in a bikini before they actually go out together; she sends one, and he doesn't write back. He presumably avoided wasting his time, while she got a familiar, cold splash of humiliation.

Unlucky preadults who start out open to love learn to blockade the doors against the emotional thieves and muggers out there. Is there anyone to trust? "You see too much betrayal, lying and infidelity," Neil Strauss, author of *The Game* and student of same, writes. "If a woman has been married three years or more, you come to learn that she's usually easier to sleep with than a single woman. If a woman has a boyfriend, you learn that you have a better chance of fucking her the night you meet her than getting her to return a phone call later."[27] Women react with understandable defensiveness. Norah Vincent, a young writer who wrote a book about her successful experience posing as a man, found that women she dated were always rubbing wounds from past relationships. Women greet men with the "presumption of guilt," she writes, so much so that "they seemed incapable of seeing any new man as an individual."[28]

Some people chalk up this bad behavior to an epidemic of generational narcissism. That's not quite right. The narcissist has excessive self-regard, or appears to; most clinicians describe their egotism, and inability to connect, as a defense against emptiness rather than as self-love. Preadults are a little different. They are neither vain nor "in love with themselves." Rather, they have learned to prize their autonomy and self-development above all. In their value system, the focused pursuit of self-interest is a feature, not a bug. Making it to the upper reaches of the knowledge economy requires mobility, independence, and radical self-involvement. Strivers are most successful when they are free agents, always ready to seize the next career move. "New York is all about change," as Carrie explains in *Sex and the City*. "[People] change their haircuts, their politics, even their friends." And of course their "relationships."

The severe autonomy required for preadulthood may suit the Single and Loving It woman and the Playboy, but it is a really hard slog for some. They have to steel themselves to it. In a "Modern Love" column of the *New York Times*, mentioned in the previous chapter, a young woman writes of trying to teach herself to adapt to preadult requirements. "I was actively seeking to practice some Zenlike form of nonattachment," she writes. "I tried to remember that no one is my property and neither am I theirs, and so I should just enjoy the time we spend together, because in the end it's our collected experiences that add up to a rich and fulfilling life. I tried to tell myself that I'm young, that this is the time to be casual, careless, lighthearted, and fun; don't ruin it."[29] Nonattachment and self-interest: these don't seem like the right groundwork for the marriages that most young people say they want, but that's what they often find themselves practicing.

It hardly needs saying that self-interest is nothing new in the mating scene. In the past, though, cold calculation was asked to hide behind an intricate carapace of rituals and manners; it might be a fact of social life, but it was an embarrassing one. No longer. Far from behaving pathologically or even rudely, "narcissistic" preadults are doing what they need to do to make it. Think of preadulthood as a profound expression of American individualism, acutely infected by the knowledge economy. It formalizes a stage of life dedicated entirely to autonomous self-exploration. Over a decade, more or less, preadults pursue the ultimate goal of self-sufficiency on their own time, setting their own schedules, determining their own biography. Even as they look for sex and companionship, they fear and resist dependence, not to mention self-negating passion. They have to.

And so, even while most educated Americans continue to be the marrying kind, there are signs that that is changing. Yes, the most recent figures show 84 percent of college-educated men marry, but that represents a decline of 9 percent since 1980. The proportion of college-educated women to have married climbed between 1950 and 1980 to 92 percent. Since then, it has declined to 86 percent.[30] Every year sees the publication of more books by single young females celebrating the life, with titles like *Singular Existence, Even God Is Single, Living Alone and Loving It,* and *The Single Girl's Manifesta: Living in a Stupendously Superior Single State of Mind.*

Of much greater significance is the rise in the number of single women having children on their own. Older, unmarried, and generally educated women who make a deliberate, planned decision to raise a child on their own refer to themselves as "choice mothers" as a way of distinguishing themselves from younger, less-educated, and unintentional single mothers. The number per thousand of unmarried mothers in their upper thirties, the likeliest age of "choice mothers," though still small, almost tripled between 1980 and 2006; this constitutes a much larger increase than rates among younger unmarried women. Coming face to face with 35, women find themselves surprised by the powerful longing for not just any child, but for their own biological offspring. Some do adopt, but more and more they go to sperm donors, either men they know or anonymous men they find through a sperm bank, a sort of father-lessness whose potential consequences for children have been largely ignored.[31]

It seems a safe bet that the number of choice mothers will continue to climb. Attitudes toward family arrangements always change slowly at first. What seems unthinkable moves to shocking, to a little strange, to respectable, to commonplace. These days, a media voracious for lifestyle oddities moves things along even faster. The outcry when a situation comedy character, the single television producer Murphy Brown, had a baby in 1992 has turned into a big yawn. Now the same woman who never could have imagined life without father only ten years ago can pick up a copy of *Knock Yourself Up: No Man? No Problem!* and *Single by Chance; Mothers by Choice*. Christine Coppa, who wrote a memoir about her pregnancy called *Rattled*, finds single motherhood to be a fabulous career starter after she gets a column at *Glamour* to describe her exciting life. She crows about "how cool it is that I managed to score a contract with a huge women's mag, pregnant and single!"[32] How cool? Really cool!

Men are sometimes irresponsible and uncommitted, crude and thoughtless, but can there be any doubt that this sort of cheering makes things worse? Before very recently, people—not just prigs and God-fearers but all civilized beings—assumed that children should have a father around. He didn't have to be around all that much. Mothers were always the primary parent, at least in the early years. In some cultures, including the United States at various points in its history, dad might be working far from home, or coming home late at night; he might not know his kids' teachers' names or even their birthdays. In less emotionally expressive cultures, it wasn't the daily routine that mattered or whether he hugged or played ball with them; it was the fact of his relationship to the child, a relationship that was considered crucial to the social order. One reason for that was that being someone's father gave men a meaningful role and identity, not to mention a reason to go to work. A boy growing up in a dad world knew something was expected of him. The culture insisted: we need you!

Today's message is more along the lines of: you're expendable! Government fatherhood initiatives and Hallmark tripe on the third Sunday of June aside, Americans have overturned the long epoch of dad. In terms of cultural attitudes, if not in absolute numbers, dads have become optional, a side dish. Now, with the growing acceptance and even celebration of anonymous sperm donation, more college-educated women are adding to the crowd of father-free homes.

Don't get me wrong. "Choice mothers" are rarely hostile to men. On the contrary. Sociologist and choice mother researcher Rosanna Hertz found that most of her non-lesbian subjects struggled for years to find husbands so they could raise their children with fathers before finally concluding they would have to go it alone. They became so "hardened through horrible dates, failed relationships, and bad timing" that they finally scratched "find husband" off the to-do list and went directly to "have baby."[33] The problem is that choice mothers tend toward a language of female empowerment that implicitly trivializes men's role in children's lives. The very term "choice mothers" frames the fatherless child as a matter of women's reproductive rights; only the woman's decision-making carries moral weight. Advocates often cite the benefits of freedom from "donor interference" that comes with single motherhood. "Single moms avoid the need to discuss and negotiate around key parenting issues," a social worker from Toronto told iParenting.com. "She can shape a child in her own unique vision."[34]

While most family researchers would disagree with them,[35] some experts are also taking a take-them-or-leave-them approach to dads. "Deconstructing the Essential Father," an article that appeared in *American Psychologist*, the flagship publication of the American Psychological Association, argued that there was simply no evidence that fathers make a difference to child outcomes. The only doubters on that score, they argued, are "neoconservative social scientists" who want to uphold "male power and privilege."[36] Peggy Drexler, assistant professor at Weill Medical College at Cornell and board member of New York University's Child Study Center, made a similar case in *Raising Boys Without Men: How Maverick Moms Are Creating the Next Generation of Exceptional Men*. Drexler makes a point of announcing that she herself is raising two children with her husband of thirty-plus years, but one has to wonder whether her book isn't a silent cry for help. Look in her index under fathers and you find "absent, after divorce," "destructive qualities of," "spending limited time with children." "In our society, often we idealize and elevate the role of father in a boy's life without giving credence to the fact that actual fathers can be destructive and a boy may be better off without his father," she informs us.[37] In Drexler's view (spoiler alert for Mr. Drexler), dadless boys are actually better, more sensitive, and more "exceptional."

And so we bump into one of the great ironies of the preadult but postfeminist age. On the one hand, the well-raised, middle-class young man learns that marriage should be a partnership of equals. He will share the cooking, cleaning, feeding, and driving so that his wife can make partner or meet her book deadline too. But he learns something else as well, something that doesn't square with that first message. He learns he is dispensable and possibly even a drag on family life. "It is, in retrospect, frightening to think how much of our sense of social order and continuity has depended on the willingness of men to succumb in the battle of the sexes; to marry, to become wage earners and to reliably share their wages with their dependents," the social critic Barbara Ehrenreich, no enthusiast for traditional familial arrangements, wrote.[38] Aren't we creating an environment where men will no longer be so willing?

The confusion about what we expect from men is perfectly captured by the existence of the sperm donor. We tell sperm donors they are performing an altruistic act, a public service for women in need. Maybe. But by going to a sperm bank, women are also unwittingly paying men to be precisely the irresponsible and crudely sex-obsessed creatures they object to. Many donors are college students—some banks accept donors as young as 18—who are simply responding to ads like that from the Fairfax Cryobank: "Why not do it for money?" Bank officials say a lot of donors are also married men who haven't bothered to mention to their wives what they're up to. David Plotz, author of *The Genius Factory*, a history of a sperm bank stocked with the sperm of Nobel Prize–winners and other geniuses, tracked down a number of the factory's donors and found a motley crew of cold-hearted rationalists, losers, and egotists—often serial donors, whom he called "The Inseminators." One of them is a sociopathic seducer with so many children through girlfriends and sperm donation that Plotz will only refer to the number as "X."[39] The donor father in the movie

The Kids Are All-Right, the story of the two children of a lesbian couple who track down their dad, turns out to be a perfect distillation of all of these cads: a pretend altruist who did it for the money and who eighteen years later remains a shallow and feckless child-man.

None of this should be taken as an excuse for the child-man's crude immaturity or his squirming alienation from the opposite sex; it is most certainly not an apology for the evil misogyny of a Roissy. Men may have lost the clarity of previous eras' scripts for growing up, but that does not mean that the only alternative is to hang out in a playground of drinking, hooking up, playing *Halo 3*, and underachieving. They can still choose to keep their eyes on the things that will lead to a meaningful life.

But we do need to recognize two big themes that should emerge from the preceding pages. First, while we have more control over our reproductive destiny, biology continues to organize life, at least for women. Biology writes a major part of the female script; you mature, meaning today you hit 30 or 35, and you reproduce—or not. For men, biology in this sense is more lax, more ill defined. It leaves doors open that are closed for women. This may be part of what the novelist Benjamin Kunkel means when he says that men are "more unfinished as people." Single motherhood only adds to the problem by creating its own negative feedback loop, as we've seen so tragically (and for admittedly many sui generis reasons) among African Americans. Too many young men resist responsible, considered adulthood. Women give up on them and go it alone. As the single mother becomes a new (almost) normal, the cultural environment becomes increasingly indifferent to a guy in the house. The result? With nobody expecting anything of them, men get worse.

The other underlying theme of this book is one easily misunderstood by Americans: the limits of individualism. Human beings are social creatures. That doesn't just mean that they like parties and Facebook or even that they want to have families. Nor does it only imply that they are inclined to help their neighbors and fellow citizens, though that's true. It means their social world shapes their understanding of the possibilities of how to live, the available life scripts, the things that might matter. People don't order or create a meaningful life out of whole cloth. They use the cultural materials available to them. The materials available to young men are meager, and what is available often contradicts itself. At bottom, they are too free, a fact epitomized by their undefined, openended, and proudly autonomous preadulthood.

The fact is, however, that the profound demographic shift toward preadulthood is not going away; the economic and cultural changes are too embedded, and for women especially, too beneficial to reverse. Still, ten or more years of dating, sexual experimentation, and confused and sometimes bruising encounters with the opposite sex have opened up fissures between men and women that need attention. Both sexes still say they want to have satisfying family lives. If that's going to happen, young women will have to get a better understanding of the limitations imposed by their bodies.

And young men? They'll need to man up.

Notes

INTRODUCTION

1. Laura Nolan, "Where Have All the Men Gone?" *Sunday Times of London*, February 1, 2008. http://women.timesonline.co.uk/tol/life_and _style/women/article3283690.ece.

2. Julie Klausner, "A Field Guide to the Bourdainians," Nerve.com, February 9, 2010. http://www.nerve.com/personalessays/klausner/field-guide-to-cool-older-men?page=2. The review of Klausner's book appears here: http://www.bookslut.com/nonfiction/2010_02_015798.php.

3. Thomas Hine, *The Rise and Fall of the American Teenager* (New York: Avon Books, 1999); Joseph Kett, *Rites of Passage: Adolescence in America 1790 to the Present* (New York: Basic Books, 1977); and Claudia Goldin and Lawrence Katz, *The Race Between Education and Technology* (Cambridge, MA: Harvard University Press, 2008), Chapter 5.

4. There is one school of thinking most notably advanced by the psychologist Jeffrey Arnett, that preadulthood represents a separate, psychological stage, much like adolescence. His ideas were explored in a much-discussed *New York Times Magazine* article. See Robin Maratz Henig, "What Is it About 20somethings?" [sic] *New York Times Magazine*, August 22, 2010. http://www.nytimes.com/2010/08/22/magazine/22Adulthood-t.html.

5. For discussion on lower-income and working-class twentysomethings, see the research from the MacArthur Transition to Adulthood study and the book based on it, *Not Quite Adults: Why 20-Somethings Are Choosing a Slower Path to Adulthood, Why It's Good for Everyone* (New York: Delacorte Press, forthcoming).

6. Marlis Buchmann, *The Script of Life in Modern Society: Entry into Adulthood in a Changing World* (Chicago: University of Chicago Press, 1989). Buchmann shows that transition to adulthood was already lengthening by the 1980s, including among those who were not pursuing a college degree.

7. Jeffrey Arnett, *Emerging Adulthood: The Winding Road from the Late Teens Through the Twenties* (New York: Oxford University Press, 2004), Chapter 10. See also Richard A. Settersten Jr., "Becoming Adult: Meaning and Markers for Young Americans," Working Papers, The Network on Transitions to Adulthood, 2006.

8. Claudia Goldin, "The Quiet Revolution That Transformed Women's Employment, Education and Family," *NBER Working Paper Series* W11953 (2006).

9. Gallup Survey, cited in Barbara Whitehead and David Popenoe, "Who Wants to Marry a Soulmate?" *The State of Our Unions* (The National Marriage Project, 2001).

10. Garey Ramey and Valerie A. Ramey, "The Rug Rat Race," Brookings Papers on Economic Activity, Spring 2010. http://econ.ucsd.edu/~vramey/research/Rugrat.pdf. The fierce résumé-building in upper-middle-class homes has an economic payoff since it appears that graduates from highly selective colleges go on to earn more than their peers from less-elite institutions.

11. Dan Kindlon, *Alpha Girls* (New York: Rodale, 2006).

12. Hanna Rosin, "The End of Men," *Atlantic Monthly*, July/August 2010: 56–72.

13. Michael Kimmel, *Guyland* (New York: HarperCollins, 2008).

14. Katherine Bindley, "The Dating Game, Ivied and Pedigreed," *New York Times*, Oct. 4, 2009.

CHAPTER ONE

1. Po Bronson, *What Should I Do With My Life?* (New York: Random House, 2002).

2. The MacArthur Network on Transitions to Adulthood at the University of Pennsylvania, a network of scholars researching the subject of preadulthood, provides one alternative moniker. Richard Setter-

sten and Barbara E. Ray use "not quite adults" in their book *Not Quite Adults: Why 20-Somethings Are Choosing a Slower Path to Adulthood, and Why It's Good for Everyone* (New York: Delacorte, 2011). See also Michel J. Rosenfeld, *The Age of Independence* (Cambridge, MA: Harvard University Press, 2007).

3. That last, which got almost no traction, was *Time*'s contribution. www.time.com/time/magazine/article/0,9171,1018089–1,00.html.

4. See, for instance, E. R. Sowell, et al., "In Vivo Evidence for Post-Adolescent Brain Maturation in Frontal and Striatal Regions," *Nature Neuroscience* 2, no. 10 (October 1999): 859–861; or J. N. Giedd, "Structural Magnetic Resonance Imaging of the Adolescent Brain," *Annals of the N.Y. Academy of Sciences* 1021 (2004): 77–85.

5. Olga Kharif, "Portland: A Magnet for Youth and Creativity," *Businessweek*, August 21, 2006. www.businessweek.com/magazine/content/06_34/b3998458.htm.

6. Empty as their pockets might seem, American preadults have more income than their counterparts in Western Europe. Lisa Bell et al., "*Failure to Launch*: Cross-National Trends in the Transition to Economic Independence," in *The Price of Independence*, ed. Sheldon Danziger and Cecilia Elena Rouse (New York: Russell Sage Foundation, 2007): 28, 31. Wages and employment levels for young men declined more in Western Europe than in the United States and the United Kingdom; in Belgium, Germany, and Italy, for instance: "employment rates of men 25 to 34 fell between 4 and 10 percentage points." By contrast, in the United States the decline was only 1 percent.

7. Peter Drucker, *Landmarks of Tomorrow: A Report on the New Postmodern World* (New York: Harper, 1959).

8. Peter Drucker, "The Age of Social Transformation," *Atlantic Monthly*, November 1994: 53–80. http://www.theatlantic.com/ideastour/markets-morals/drucker-full.html.

9. Ian D. Wyatt and Daniel E. Hecker, "Occupational Changes During the 20th Century," *Monthly Labor Review* 129, no. 3 (March 2006). www.bls.gov/opub/mlr/2006/03/art3full.pdf.

10. National Center for Education Statistics, "Earned Degrees in Business Conferred by Degree-Granting Institutions," Table 284, August 2001. http://nces.ed.gov/pubs2002/digest2001/tables/dt284.as.

11. Richard Florida, *The Rise of the Creative Class* (New York: Basic Books, 2002), 75.

12. There is lively debate about whether higher education is really as necessary in today's economy as people seem to believe. See, for instance, http://chronicle.com/article/Are-Too-Many-Students-Going-to/49039/. A number of critics believe that college has nothing to do with knowledge and everything to do with "signaling." The economist/blogger Robin Hanson discusses the issue frequently at his blog overcomingbias .com. Barbara Schneider and David Stevenson, *The Ambitious Generation: America's Teenagers Motivated but Directionless* (New Haven, Yale University Press, 1999), 33, 82, also argue that teens tend to overstate the benefits of a college degree.

13. Goldin and Katz (see Introduction, note 3) demonstrate that the biggest gains in college attainment came in the 1970s and early 1980s and it hasn't increased much since then.

14. Nicole S. Stoops, "A Half Century of Learning: Historical Statistics on Educational Attainment in the United States 1940–2000." U.S. Census Bureau, Population Division, http://www.census.gov/population/ www/socdemo/education/introphct41.html.

15. Drucker, "The Age of Social Transformation."

16. Census Bureau, "Educational Attainment in the United States," 2007. www.census.gov/population/www/socdemo/educ-attn.html. Also see Allstate/National Journal Heartland Monitor Poll, January 3–7, 2010. www.nationaljournal.com/img/topline100114.pdf.

17. Schneider and Stevenson, 75. Nathan E. Bell, "Graduate Enrollment and Degrees, 1997–2007," Council of Graduate Schools, Washington, DC, 2008. www.cgsnet.org/portals/0/pdf/R_ED2007.pdf.

18. Katherin Peter and Laura Horn, "Gender Differences in Participation and Completion of Undergraduate Education and How They Have Changed Over Time," National Center for Education Statistics, February 2005. http://nces.ed.gov/pubsearch/pubsinfo.asp?pubid=2005169.

19. Richard Whitmore, *Why Boys Fail* (New York: Amacon, 2010).

20. Gary S. Becker, William H. J. Hubbard, and Kevin M. Murphy, "The Market for College Graduates and the Worldwide Boom in Higher Education of Women," *American Economic Review* 100, no. 2 (2010): 229–233.

21. U.S. Census Bureau, "Educational Attainment in the United States, 2007"; and Ruben G. Rumbaut and Golnaz Komai, "Young Adults in the United States: A Mid-Decade Profile," *Network on Transitions to Adulthood Research Network Working Paper*, 2007. See also Lisa Barrow and Cecilia Rouse, "Does College Still Pay?" *The Economists's Voice* 2, no.4 (2005).

22. David Autor, "The Polarization of Job Opportunities in the U.S. Labor Market," The Hamilton Project, Center for American Progress, April 2010.

23. Don Lee, "Is a College Degree Worth It?" *Los Angeles Times*, June 12, 2010. www.latimes.com/business/la-fi-jobs-educate-20100612,0,546 6021,full.story. See also Sarah Kaufman, "Some Say Bypassing College Is Better Than Paying for a Degree," *Washington Post*, September 10, 2010. www.washingtonpost.com/wp-dyn/content/article/2010/09/09/AR2010090903350.html?hpid=topnews.

24. There's significant disagreement about just how burdensome student loan debt is for this generation. See Tamara Draut, *Strapped* (New York: Doubleday, 2006) versus The American Council on Education's 2004 report "Debt Burden: Repaying Student Debt," which found that much of the increase in debt is from students with well-to-do families who now have more access to loans because of the 1992 Higher Education Act. See also Danziger and Rouse.

25. Settersten and Ray, Chapter 1.

26. Peter Coy, "The Lost Generation," *Businessweek*, October 8, 2009. www.businessweek.com/magazine/content/09_42/b4151032038302.htm.

27. Richard Florida, "25 Best Cities for College Grads," *The Daily Beast*, May 26, 2010. www.thedailybeast.com/blogs-and-stories/2010 -05-26/best-cities-for-college-graduates-from-ithaca-to-seattle/full/. For the international story of changes in the labor market for young workers, see Hans-Peter Blossfeld et al., *Globalization, Uncertainty and Youth in Society* (New York: Routledge, 2009).

28. James Manyika, "The Coming Imperative for the World's Knowledge Economy," *Financial Times*, May 16, 2006. Reprinted at www .mckinsey.com/aboutus/mckinseynews/knowledge_economy.asp. See also Anthony Carnevale, Nicole Smith, and Jeff Strohl, "Help Wanted: Projections of Jobs and Education Requirements Through 2018," Center on

Education and the Workforce, Georgetown University, June 2010. http://cew.georgetown.edu/JOBS2018/.

29. Alex Altman, "High Tech, High Touch, High Growth," *Time*, May 14, 2009. www.time.com/time/specials/packages/article/0,28804 ,1898024_1898023_1898101,00.html.

30. http://nextgenerationworkplace.blogspot.com/2006_01_01_archive .html.

31. Lisa Chamberlain, *Slackonomics: Generation X in the Age of Creative Destruction* (New York: Da Capo Press, 2008), 47.

32. Peter Orszag, "Salary Statistics," Office of Management and Budget post on whitehouse.gov, March 10, 2010. www.whitehouse.gov/omb/ blog/10/03/10/Salary-Statistics/.

33. Bureau of Labor Statistics, U.S. Department of Labor, "Career Guide to Industries, 2010–2011," Federal Government. www.bls.gov/ oco/cg/cgs041.htm.

34. National Center for Charitable Statistics, "Number of Nonprofit Organizations in the United States, 1998–2008," Urban Institute. http:// nccsdataweb.urban.org/PubApps/profile1.php?state=US; and www.ur-ban.org/publications/901011.html.

35. National Center for Education Statistics, Table 2006. Digest of Education Statistics, 2008. http://nces.ed.gov/programs/digest/d08/tables/ dt08_206.asp.

36. "Law School Faculties 40% Larger Than 10 Years Ago," *National Jurist*, March 9, 2010. www.nationaljurist.com/content/law-school-faculties -40-larger-10-years-ago.

37. Data from United States Census Bureau, cited in Katie Adams, "50 Years of Consumer Spending," Financial Edge on investodpedia.com, October 15, 2009. http://financialedge.investopedia.com/financial-edge/ 1009/50-Years-Of-Consumer-Spending.aspx.

38. "CLIA's 35th Anniversary Puts Spotlight on Remarkable Story of Growth and Evolution of Cruise Industry," Hospitality Trends.com, March 17, 2010. www.htrends.com/article44451CLIA_S___TH_Anniversary _Puts_Spotlight_on_Remarkable_Story_of_Growth___Evolution_of _Cruise_Industry.html.

39. Joseph Lewis Ettle, "Irrational Exuberance: Calculating the Total Number of Museums in the United States" (dissertation, Baylor Uni-

versity, 2006). https://beardocs.baylor.edu/bitstream/2104/4196/1/joseph
_ettle_masters.pdf.

40. *Occupational Outlook Handbook, 2010–2011*, "Archivists, Curators, and Museum Technicians," www.bls.gov/oco/ocos065.htm.

41. National Endowment for the Arts, "All America's a Stage: Growth
and Challenges in Nonprofit Theater," 2008. http://arts.endow.gov/
research/TheaterBrochure12-08.pdf. See also Richard Zoglin, "Bigger
Than Broadway!" *Time*, May 27, 2003. www.time.com/time/magazine/
article/0,9171,454479-2,00.html.

42. United States Census Bureau, 2002 Economic Census; Industry
Series, www.census.gov/econ/industry/ec02/e812990.htm.

43. Vinay Couto et al. "The Globalization of White Collar Work: The
Facts and Fallout of Next Generation Offshoring," The Duke Fuqua
School of Business and Booz Allen Hamilton, 2006. www.boozallen.com/
media/file/Globalization_White_Collar_Work_v3.pdf.

44. See this oft-quoted research from Lisa B. Kahn, "The Long Term
Labor Market Consequences of Graduating College in a Bad Economy,"
Labor Economics 17 no. 2 (April 2010). Jim Pinto argues that an in-
creasing number of high-skilled jobs will be moving offshore as college
graduation rates rise in developing economies. "The New Global Job
Shift," *InTech*, May 2003. www.isa.org/Content/ContentGroups/
News/20031/May19/InTech15/Pintos_Point__The_new_global_job
_shift.htm.

45. Xianglei Chen and Thomas Weko, "Students Who Study Science, Technology, Engineering and Mathematics in Postsecondary Education," National Center for Education Statistics, July 2009. http://nces
.ed.gov/pubs2009/2009161.pdf.

46. Peter R. Drucker, "Managing Oneself," *Harvard Business Review*
107 (January 2005).

47. Arnett, see Introduction, note 7, 146.

48. Derek Thompson, "Millennials Chasing Their Dreams, By Necessity." *National Journal*, May 8, 2010. www.nationaljournal.com/nj
magazine/nj_20100508_4630.php.

49. Don Peck, "Early Career Moves Are Most Important," *National
Journal*, May 8, 2010. www.nationaljournal.com/njmagazine/nj_20100
508_6198.php.

50. Henry Faber, "Is The Company Man an Anachronism? Trends in Long-Term Employment in the United States," in Danziger and Rouse.

51. Scott Adams, "Career Advice," Dilbertblog, July 20, 2007. http://dilbertblog.typepad.com/the_dilbert_blog/2007/07/career-advice.html.

52. Amy Kass and Leon Kass, eds., *Wing to Wing, Oar to Oar: Readings on Courting and Marrying* (Notre Dame, IN: University of Notre Dame Press, 2000), 1.

53. Alexandra Levit, *How'd You Score That Gig? A Guide to the Coolest Jobs and How to Get Them* (New York: Ballantine Books, 2008).

54. This is at odds with surveys cited by Settersten and Ray showing millennials wanting work to play a less central role in their lives, 59–60.

55. Alexandra Robbins and Abby Wilner, *Quarterlife Crisis* (New York: Tarcher, 2001), 78.

56. Nadira A. Hira, "Attracting the Twentysomething Worker," May 15, 2007. Reprinted at money.cnn.com/magazines/fortune/fortune_archive/2007/05/28/100033934/index.htm.

57. See especially Jean Twenge, *Generation Me* (New York: Free Press, 2006).

58. For a more pessimistic view of the gratifications of knowledge work, see Matthew B. Crawford, *Shop Class as Soulcraft: An Inquiry into the Value of Work* (New York: Penguin, 2009); and Richard Sennett, *The Corrosion of Character: The Personal Consequences of Work in the New Capitalism* (New York: Norton, 1998).

59. Peter Joseph Kuhn and Fernando Luzano, "The Expanding Workweek? Understanding Trends in Long Work Hours Among U.S. Men, 1979–2004," *Journal of Labor Economics* 2, no. 4 (2008), 311–343. Between 1980 and 2001, the proportion of college-educated men working fifty hours or more climbed from 22.2 percent to 30.5 percent.

60. "The American Freshman, National Norms 2009," Research Brief, Higher Education Research Institute, January 2010.

61. Bronson, 47. See also Paul D. Tieger and Barbara Barron-Tieger's popular career guide *Do What You Are* (Boston: Little, Brown, 2001).

62. Robbins and Wilner. See also Alexandra Robbins, *Conquering Your Quarterlife Crisis* (New York: Perigree Trade, 2004).

63. Ben Casnocha, "The Quarterlife Crisis," Ben Casnocha blog, May 20, 2009. http://ben.casnocha.com/2009/05/the-quarter-life-crisis.html.

64. Fajita's Blog, "Confessions of Emerging Adulthood," July 21, 2009. http://homefront.blogspot.com/.

65. Florida, 155.

66. Christine Whalen, *Why Smart Men Marry Smart Women* (New York: Simon & Schuster, 2006).

67. D'Vera Cohn, "The States of Marriage and Divorce," Pew Research Center Reports, October 15, 2009. http://pewsocialtrends.org/pubs/746/states-of-marriage-and-divorce.

68. Frank F. Furstenberg Jr. et al., "Growing Up Is Harder to Do," *Contexts* 3, no. 3 (2004): 33–41. http://contexts.org/docs/furstenberg.pdf. See also Arnett, 209ff.

69. Rosenfeld, 53.

70. Bell. Italian men score lowest in this area; in 2000, only 40 percent were household heads.

71. Don Peck, "How a New Jobless Era Will Transform America," *The Atlantic Monthly*, March 2010.

72. Aaron Yelowitz. "Young Adults Leaving the Nest," in Danziger and Rouse, 170–206. Yelowitz finds that any increase in the number of young adults living with their parents had little to do with housing costs. Those costs started to rise in the early 2000s, and yet during those years there was no increase in the percentage of kids moving home.

73. Gordon Berlin, Frank F. Furstenberg Jr., and Mary C. Waters, "Introducing the Issue," *The Future of Children* 20, no. 1 (Spring 2010): 6.

74. It is true, however, that many parents help out financially, even if their adult children are not living at home. See Robert F. Schoeni and Karen E. Ross, "Material Assistance from Families During the Transition to Adulthood," in *On the Frontier of Adulthood*, eds. Richard A. Settersten Jr. et al. (Chicago: University of Chicago Press, 2005), 396.

75. Rosenfeld, Chapter 3. See also Yelowitz, 176; and Frances K. Goldscheider and Calvin Goldscheider, "Moving Out and Marriage: What Do Young Adults Expect?" *American Sociological Review* 52 (1987): 278–285.

76. Wendy Wang and Rich Morin, "Home for the Holidays—and Every Other Day," Pew Research Center Reports, November 24, 2009. http://pewsocialtrends.org/pubs/748/recession-brings-many-young-adults-back-to-the-nest#prc-jump.

77. *New York Times Real Estate* magazine, Fall 2007.

78. See Ethan Watters, *Urban Tribes: Are Friends the New Family?* (New York: Bloomsbury USA, 2003).

CHAPTER TWO

1. Li Yuan, "Chinese Views of *Sex and the City*," *Wall Street Journal*, June 16, 2008. http://online.wsj.com/article/SB121303574217257923 .html.

2. "Women earn 77 cents for every dollar earned by men," is the way it is usually put. But because this formula doesn't take into account differences in vocational fields, job interruptions, or hours worked, what it really amounts to is a statement that 1. women work fewer hours than men and take more time off; and 2. nurses earn less than doctors, and pediatricians less than surgeons—and that more women than men become nurses and pediatricians. When comparing apples to apples, that is, surgeons to surgeons, researchers find evidence for only a very small gap—5 percent or less—that might or might not be explained by discrimination. See this report undertaken for the Labor Department concluding that women earn 94 cents on the dollar: www.consad.com/content/ reports/Gender%20Wage%20Gap%20Final%20Report.pdf. This study from the Bureau of Labor Statistics finds that young women aged 16 to 24 have median salaries that were 91 percent of those of men in 2008: www.dol.gov/wb/stats/main.htm. "Behind the Pay Gap," a 2007 study by the American Association of University Women (AAUW), looked at recent college graduates, the childless, and those working full-time. The report concluded that women earn only 80 percent of that earned by similar men. However, the report generalizes occupations in ways that probably distort their findings. For instance, the researchers find a large pay gap in "health professions." But as already noted, women tend to choose less lucrative niches in medicine than men. www.aauw.org/learn/ research/upload/behindPayGap.pdf.

3. Sheldon Danziger and David Ratner, "Labor Market Outcomes and the Transition to Adulthood," *The Future of Children* 20, no. 1 (Spring 2010): 141.

4. U.S. Department of Education, "Degrees Conferred by Degree Granting Institutions by Level of Degree and Sex of Student," Table 268. Digest of Education Statistics. http://nces.ed.gov/programs/digest/d09/tables/dt09_268.asp. See also Tamar Lewin, "At Colleges, Women Are Leaving Men in the Dust," *New York Times*, July 9, 2006. www.nytimes.com/2006/07/09/education/09college.html?pagewanted=2&_r=1&adxnnl=1&adxnnlx=1285002233-b1uy43ej232YdAcaecl6tg.

5. Britney L. Moraski, "The New Gender Gap: Are Men the Endangered Species on College Campuses?" *The Harvard Crimson*, June 7, 2006. www.thecrimson.com/article/2006/6/7/the-new-gender-gap-when-elizabeth/.

6. There are four all-male schools in the United States, none of them with the cachet of these women's colleges. One, Morehouse, is an African American university; another, St. John's, is a Catholic one.

7. "The MetLife Survey of the American Teacher, Part Two, Student Achievement." MetLife Inc., 2009. www.metlife.com/assets/cao/contributions/foundation/american-teacher/MetLife_Teacher_Survey_2009_Part_2.pdf.

8. College Board, "The Fourth Annual AP Report to the Nation," 2008. http://professionals.collegeboard.com/profdownload/ap-report-to-the-nation-2008.pdf.

9. College Board, "Total Group Profile Report," 2009. http://professionals.collegeboard.com/profdownload/cbs-2009-national-TOTAL-GROUP.pdf.

10. National Center for Education Statistics, "Youth Indicators, 2005" Indicator 18: Educational Aspirations. http://nces.ed.gov/programs/youthindicators/Indicators.asp?PubPageNumber=18&ShowTablePage=TablesHTML/18.asp.

11. Daniel DeVise, "Sex Bias Probe in Colleges' Selection," *Washington Post*, December 14, 2009. www.washingtonpost.com/wp-dyn/content/article/2009/12/13/AR2009121302922.html. Also see "Probe of Extra Help for Men," *Inside Higher Education*, November 2, 2009. www.insidehighered.com/news/2009/11/02/admit.

12. Jennifer Delahunty Britz, "To All the Girls I've Rejected," *New York Times*, op ed, March 23, 2006. The problem is especially acute at

second-tier colleges. At the most elite schools, such as Harvard, you will always have enough applicants of both sexes to make an exceptional class. Not so much at such places as Vassar, Skidmore, or Bowdoin.

13. Richard Whitmire, "Boy Trouble Hits College Admissions," EducationNews.org, December 18, 2009. www.educationnews.org/educationnewstoday/11586.html. See also Sandy Baum and Eban Goodstein, "Gender Imbalance in College Applications: Does It Lead to a Preference for Men in the Admissions Process?" *Economics of Education Review* 24, no. 6 (2005): 665–675. This article found that in selective liberal arts colleges, being male increases the chance of acceptance by 6.5 to 9 percentage points.

14. Jillian Kinze et al., "The Relationship Between Gender and Student Engagement in College," www.womenscolleges.org/files/pdfs/Gender-and-Student-Engagement-in-College.pdf.

15. "Women Abroad and Men at Home," *Inside Higher Education*, December 4, 2008. www.insidehighered.com/news/2008/12/04/genderabroad. See also Peter Schmidt, "Men and Women Differ in How They Decide to Study Abroad, Study Finds," *The Chronicle of Higher Education*, November 6, 2009. http://chronicle.com/article/MenWomen-Differ-in-How/49085/.

16. "So What Did You Learn in London?" *Insider Higher Education*, June 1, 2007. www.insidehighered.com/news/2007/06/01/research.

17. Sara Lipka, "To Get More Men to Volunteer, Colleges Must Make an Extra Effort," *Chronicle of Higher Education*, March 9, 2010. http://chronicle.com/article/To-Get-More-Men-to-Volunteer/64579/.

18. Richard Whitmire, Why Boys Fail blog, *Education Week*, February 2010. http://blogs.edweek.org/edweek/whyboysfail/2010/02/men_of_merit_in_college.html?utm_source=feedburner&utm_medium=feed&utm_campaign=Feed%3A+WhyBoysFail+%28Why+Boys+Fail%29&utm_content=Google+Feedfetcher.

19. J. S. Wirt et al., "The Condition of Education 2004," U.S. Department of Education, National Center for Education Statistics.

20. AAUW, "Behind the Pay Gap." (See note 2.)

21. Barbara Dafoe Whitehead, *Why There Are No Good Men Left* (New York: Broadway Books, 2003), 67.

22. Cited in Kindlon; (see Introduction, note 11), based on Catalyst Census data, 191, 196.

23. National Center for Education Statistics, Fast Facts, Percentage of Degrees by Sex and Race, http://nces.ed.gov/fastfacts/display.asp?id=72. Also see "Women Lead in Doctorates," *Insider Higher Education*, September 14, 2010. http://www.insidehighered.com/news/2010/09/14/doctorates.

24. National Center for Education Statistics, Fast Facts. Information on College Enrollment. http://nces.ed.gov/fastFacts/display.asp?id=98.

25. Francesca Di Meglio, "Breaking B-School Gender Barriers," *Businessweek*, September 10, 2010. www.businessweek.com/bschools/content/dec2004/bs2004121_4063.htm.

26. "Forté Foundation Member Schools Showing Significant Gains in Women's MBA Enrollment," Press Release, Forté Foundation, October 11, 2006. http://www.fortefoundation.org/site/DocServer/Gainsin MBA_Enrollment.pdf?docID=4032.

27. Sam Roberts, "For Young Earners, a Gap in Women's Favor," *New York Times*, August 8, 2007. www.nytimes.com/2007/08/03/nyregion/03 women.html?pagewanted=print.

28. Belinda Luscombe, "Workplace Salaries: At Last Women on Top," *Time*, September 1, 2010. www.time.com/time/business/article/0,8599 ,2015274,00.html.

29. See AAUW, above, for female education, psychology, and engineering majors. For computer science, see National Center for Women and Information Technology, "By the Numbers," www.ncwit.org/pdf/ BytheNumbers09.pdf. See also Judith McDonald and Robert J. Thornton, "Do New Male and Female Graduates Receive Equal Pay?" *Journal of Human Resources* 42, no. 1 (2007).

30. Marianne Betrand, Claudia Goldin, and Lawrence F. Katz, "Dynamics of the Gender Gap for Young Professionals in the Financial and Corporate Sector," *NBER Working Paper* 14681 (2009). www.economics .harvard.edu/faculty/katz/files/Dynamics.pdf.

31. AAUW. *Forbes* lists the highest-paid college majors, almost all of them involving computers and numbers, as computer engineering, electrical engineering, computer science, and finance. Kurt Badenhausen, "Most Lucrative College Majors," *Forbes*, June 18, 2008. www.forbes.com/ 2008/06/18/college-majors-lucrative-lead-cx_kb_0618majors.html.

32. Laura Rowley, "The Single Woman and Real Estate," *Yahoo Finance*, December 7, 2006. http://finance.yahoo.com/expert/article/

moneyhappy/17039. See also "Single Women Outpace Single Men in Real Estate Market," Marketwatch, *Wall Street Journal*, May 9, 2010.

33. Eurostat, "The Life of Women and Men in Europe: A Statistical Portrait," European Commission, 2008. http://epp.eurostat.ec.europa .eu/cache/ITY_OFFPUB/KS-80-07-135/EN/KS-80-07-135-EN.PDF.

34. Charla Griffy-Brown and Noriko Oakland, "Women Entrepreneurship," *Griziadio Business Reports* 10 no. 1 (2007). http://gbr.pepperdine .edu/071/japan.html.

35. "World Fertility Patterns 2009," Department of Economic and Social Affairs, Population Division, United Nations, 2010. For Japan, see Carl Haub, "Japan's Demographic Future," Population Reference Bureau, Washington, DC, 2010. www.prb.org/Articles/2010/japandemography .aspx. For Korea, see Korea National Statistical Office, cited in http:// paa2007.princeton.edu/download.aspx?submissionId=7203. More generally, see Ron Lesthaeghe, "The Unfolding Story of the Second Demographic Transition," *Population and Development Review* 36, no. 2 (June 16, 2010): 211–251.

36. Yoon Ja-yung, "20% of Women in Early Thirties Remain Single," *The Korea Times*, October 11, 2009. www.koreatimes.co.kr/www/news/ nation/2009/12/117_53296.html.

37. David Rimer and Stephanie Steinmetz, "Gender Differentiation in Higher Education in Spain and Germany," *Working Paper* 99, MZES, University of Manheim, 2007. www.mzes.uni-mannheim.de/publications/ wp/wp-99.pdf.

38. Yuan. http://online.wsj.com/article/SB121303574217257923.html.

39. For a more extended discussion, see my "New Girl Order," *City Journal*, Autumn 2007.

40. Martha J. Bailey, "More Power to the Pill: The Impact of Contraceptive Freedom on Women's Labor-Force Participation," *Vanderbilt University Economics Working Paper No. 04-WG01R* (July 2005). Available at SSRN: http://ssrn.com/abstract=652521.

41. Claudia Goldin, Lawrence F. Katz, and Ilyana Kuziemko, "The Homecoming of American College Women," *Journal of Economic Perspectives* 20, no. 4 (Fall 2006): 133–156. www.economics.harvard.edu/ faculty/goldin/files/homecoming.pdf.

42. Center for Disease Control and Prevention, "Contraceptive Use," FastStats. www.cdc.gov/nchs/fastats/usecontr.htm.

43. Goldin and Katz also mention antidiscrimination laws, a rising college wage premium, and the prevalence of divorce.

44. Paul C. Glick, "Updating the Life Cycle of the Family," *Journal of Marriage and Family* 39 (1977): 5–13.

45. Stefania Albanesi and Claudia Olivetti, "Gender Roles and Technological Progress," *NBER Working Paper* 13179 (2007).

46. Centers for Disease Control. "Achievements in Public Health, 1900–1999: Healthier Mothers and Babies," *MMWR Weekly*, October 1, 1999. www.cdc.gov/mmwr/preview/mmwrhtml/mm4838a2.htm.

47. See, for instance, Heidi Hartmann, "Capitalism, Patriarchy, and Job Segregation by Sex," *Signs* 1, no. 3 (1976); and "Capitalism, Patriarchy, and the Subordination of Women," in *Social Class and Stratification*, ed. Rhonda Levine (Lanham, MD: Rowman and Littlefield, 2006), Chapter 10.

48. Janet Farrell Brodie, *Contraception and Abortion in 19th Century America* (Ithaca, NY: Cornell University Press, 1994), 209ff.

49. Gail Collins, *When Everything Changed: The Amazing Journey of American Women from 1960 to the Present* (Boston: Little, Brown, 2009), 102.

50. Albanesi and Olivetti, 2.

51. Joel Mokyr, *The Gifts of Athena: Historical Origins of the Knowledge Economy* (Princeton, NJ: Princeton University Press, 2002), 209.

52. Betty Friedan, *The Feminine Mystique* (New York: Norton, 1963), 333.

53. Joel Mokyr, "Why Is There More Work for Mother? Knowledge and Household Behavior 1870–1945." *Journal of Economic History* 60, no. 1 (March 2000): 1–40.

54. Leslie T. Chang, *Factory Girls* (New York: Spiegel and Grau, 2008).

55. Jeremy Greenwood, Ananth Seshadri, and Mehmet Yorukoglu, "Engines of Liberation," *Review of Economic Studies* 72, no. 1 (2005), 109–133. www.jeremygreenwood.net/papers/engines.pdf.

56. Collins, 43–44.

57. Greenwood et al. This paper finds that household revolution explains half of the rise in female labor force participation between 1900 and 1980, when 50 percent of married women were in the workforce. Between 1940 and 1960, participation rates for women under 35 actually declined, but that of older women with school-age children increased substantially. See also Emanuela Cardia and Paul Gomme, "The Household Revolution" (unpublished paper, 2009). Available at https://editorial express.com/cgi-bin/conference/download.cgi?db_name=SED2010&paper_id=1000.

58. Joel Mokyr, "The Second Industrial Revolution, 1970–1914," in *Storia dell'economia Mondiale*, ed. Valerio Castronovo (Rome: Laterza Publishing, 1999). http://faculty.wcas.northwestern.edu/~jmokyr/castronovo.pdf.

59. Adams, see Chapter 1, note 37. http://financialedge.investopedia.com/financial-edge/1009/50-Years-Of-Consumer-Spending.aspx.

60. The irony is that, despite the pill, out-of-wedlock childbearing soared among those with less than a college degree. See my *Marriage and Caste in America* (Chicago: Ivan R. Dee, 2006).

61. Friedan, 344.

62. H. Haygyhe, "Women's Labor Force Trends and Women's Transportation Issues," Bureau of the Census, www.fhwa.dot.gov/ohim/womens/chap1.pdf.

63. Allyson Sherman Grossman, "More Than Half of All Children Have Working Mothers," Special Labor Force Reports, Monthly Labor Review, February 1982, 41–43.

64. Whitehead.

65. Kindlon, 33–34.

66. Ibid.

67. *State of Our Unions*, 2001, The National Marriage Project.

68. Twenge (see Chapter 1, note 57), 193, 195.

69. Elizabeth Seale and Barbara Risman, "Betwixt and Between: Gender Contradictions in Middle School," in *Families as They Really Are*, ed. Barbara Risman (New York: Norton, 2009).

70. Kindlon, xv.

71. Carol Gilligan and Lyn Mikel Brown, *Meeting at the Crossroads* (Cambridge, MA: Harvard University Press, 1992), 88.

72. Elizabeth Debold, Marie C. Wilson, and Idelisse Malave, *Mother Daughter Revolution* (New York: Da Capo Press, 1993), x.

73. The Women's Bureau of the United States Department of Labor, 1993.

74. Sandra Stotsky, *Losing Our Language* (New York: Encounter Books, 2002), 83.

75. See also Anita Harris, *Future Girl: Young Women in the Twenty-First Century* (London: Routledge, 2003); and Sherrie A. Inness, *Action Chicks: New Images of Tough Women in Pop Culture* (Hampshire: Palgrave MacMillan, 2004).

76. See also Christina Hoff Sommers, *The War Against Boys* (New York: Simon & Schuster, 2000).

77. For a jaundiced view of these trends, see Benjamin DeMott, *Killer Woman Blues* (New York: Houghton Mifflin Harcourt, 2000).

78. Eleanor Mills, "Learning to Be Left on the Shelf," *The Sunday Times*, April 18, 2010. www.timesonline.co.uk/tol/comment/columnists/guest_contributors/article7100770.ece.

79. Lori Gottlieb, *Marry Him* (New York: Dutton Adult, 2010), 55.

80. Girls Inc. "The Supergirl Dilemma: Girls Grapple With the Mounting Pressure of Expectations," 2006. www.girlsinc.org/supergirl dilemma/.

81. Sara Rimer, "For Girls, It's Be Yourself, and Be Perfect, Too," *New York Times*, April 1, 2007. www.nytimes.com/2007/04/01/education/01girls.html?_r=1. See also Liz Funk, *Supergirls Speak Out: Inside the Secret Crisis of Overachieving Girls* (New York: Touchstone, 2009), by a 20-year-old who laments that it took so long for her to publish her first book.

82. Michelle Conlin, "The New Gender Gap," *Businessweek*, May 21, 2003. www.businessweek.com/magazine/content/03_21/b3834001_mz001.htm.

83. Mark J. Perry, "The Increasing College Degree Gap: Will College Women's Centers Address This Issue?" Carpe Diem blog, April 11, 2010. http://mjperry.blogspot.com/2010/04/update-on-increasing-college-degree-gap.html.

84. Susan Douglas, *Enlightened Sexism* (New York: Times Books, 2010), 85.

85. Ruth Shalit Barett, "Girl Crazy," *Elle*, October 2009. Reprinted at www.freerepublic.com/focus/news/2364183/posts.

86. John Gravois, "Bringing Up Babes," Slate.com, January 16, 2004. www.slate.com/id/2093899/. See also Rosin, Introduction, note 12, 56–58.

87. Choe Sang-Hun, "Where Boys Were Kings, A Shift Towards Baby Girls," *New York Times*, December 23, 2007. www.nytimes.com/2007/12/23/world/asia/23skorea.html?_r=2&hp=&oref=slogin&pagewanted=all.

88. Kindlon, 30.

CHAPTER THREE

1. Friedan (see Chapter 2, note 52), 121.

2. Chang (see Chapter 2, note 54), 188.

3. Ibid., 207.

4. Goldin (see Introduction, note 8).

5. Collins (see Chapter 2, note 49).

6. Ibid., 49.

7. "Female Power," *The Economist*, December 30, 2009. Reprinted at www.activeboard.com/forum.spark?aBID=132683&p=3&topicID=33170265.

8. A disproportionate number of men work in higher-risk occupations; those occupations are typically compensated with higher pay. Coal mining is almost 100 percent male, firefighters 96.6 percent, police officers 84.5 percent, and correctional officers 73.1 percent. There are almost no female crane and tower operators, roofers, or roustabouts. Bureau of Labor Statistics, "Household Data Annual Averages," Chart 11, 2009. www.bls.gov/cps/cpsaat11.pdf. See also Kate O'Beirne, *Women Who Make the World Worse* (New York: Sentinel Trade Books, 2006).

9. Connie Schultz, "Promise in a Lunch Pail," *The Plain Dealer*, May 8, 2007.

10. See, for instance, Robert B. Reich, *The Future of Success* (New York: Knopf, 2001).

11. Ibid., 39.

12. Federal Reserve Bank of Dallas, "The Evolution of Work," 2003 Annual Report, 21. www.dallasfed.org/fed/annual/2003/ar03f.pdf.

13. Ibid., 20.

14. "Women in the Labor Force: A Data Book, 2009 Edition." Labor Force Statistics from the Current Population Survey, Bureau of Labor Force Statistics, 2009. www.bls.gov/cps/wlf-intro-2009.htm.

15. United States Department of Labor, Women's Bureau, "Quick Stats on Women Workers, 2009." www.dol.gov/wb/stats/main.htm. As in the past, women are the majority of elementary, middle, and secondary school teachers and registered nurses, as well as physical therapists.

16. For a fuller exposition on this theme, see my "Portrait of the Artist as a Young Businesswoman," *City Journal*, Spring 2009. www.city-journal.org/2009/19_2_visual-designers.html.

17. Interview with author, February 2009.

18. Richard Lloyd, *Neo-Bohemia: Art and Commerce in the Postindustrial City* (New York: Routledge, 2006), 219 [italics in original].

19. Quoted in "The iPad Launch: Can Steve Jobs Do It Again?" *Time*, April 1, 2010. www.time.com/time/business/article/0,8599,1976935-4,00.html.

20. Virginia Postrel, *The Substance of Style* (New York: HarperCollins, 2003), 47.

21. Ibid.

22. Daniel Pink, *A Whole New Mind* (New York: Riverhead Books, 2005), 54.

23. Phone interview with author, February 2009.

24. In 2008, only 18 percent of graduating computer majors were women. That was down from 37 percent in 1985. National Center for Women and Information Technology (see Chapter 2, note 29).

25. Ann Zimmerman, "Revenge of the Nerds: How Barbie Got Her Geek On," *Wall Street Journal*, April 9, 2010.

26. Sarah Bernard, "The Perfect Prescription," *New York Magazine*, May 21, 2005.

27. Tom Peters, "Dispatches," Tompeters.com, www.tompeters.com/dispatches/design/.

28. See The Yankee Candle Company, Company History.

29. http://hbr.org/2009/09/the-female-economy/ar/1.

30. "Singles and the City: The Bridget Jones Economy," *The Economist*, December 20, 2001.

31. Quoted in Anne Kingston, *The Meaning of Wife* (New York: Farrar, Straus and Giroux, 2004), 204.

32. Quoted in Joanne Cleaver, "What Women Want," *Entrepreneur*, February 2004. Reprinted at http://findarticles.com/p/articles/mi_m0DTI/is_2_32/ai_112686130/pg_3/. In Japan, young women do so much shopping—and traveling—that at least five magazines aimed at this crowd begin publication each year. See "Women Entrepreneurship," *Griziadio Business Reports* 10, no. 1 (2007). http://gbr.pepperdine.edu/071/japan.html.

33. "What's Behind the Surge in Women Entrepreneurs: Interview with Ernst and Young's Gregory Eriksen," *Businessweek*, July 15,1999. www.businessweek.com/smallbiz/news/coladvice/trends/tr990715.htm.

34. Chloe Dao, "About," Chloedao.com, www.chloedao.com/dcd/about.php.

35. Barbara F. Reskin and Patricia A. Roos, *Job Queues, Gender Queues* (Philadelphia: Temple University Press, 1990), 13.

36. Nathaniel Hawthorne in an 1855 letter to his British publisher, cited in *Hawthorne and Women*, ed. John L. Idol Jr. and Melinda M. Ponder (Boston: University of Massachusetts Press, 1999), 21.

37. Jessica Bennett, Jesse Ellison, and Sarah Ball, "Are We There Yet?" *Newsweek*, March 18, 2010.

38. Bookstatistics.com. http://parapublishing.com/sites/para/resources/statistics.cfm.

39. Reskin and Roos, Chapter 4.

40. Collins, 269.

41. Preethi Dumpala, "The Year the Newspaper Died," *Business Insider*, July 4, 2009.

42. Cited at Bookstatistics.com.

43. "2008 Enrollment Report," Annual Surveys of Journalism and Mass Communication, Grady College, University of Georgia, 2008. www.grady.uga.edu/annualsurveys/Enrollment_Survey/Enrollment_2008/Enroll2008cover&supplemental%20tabs.pdf.

44. Laura Streib, "Journalism Bust, J-School Boom," *Forbes*, April 6, 2009. www.forbes.com/2009/04/06/journalism-media-jobs-business-media

-jobs.html. See also "2008 Enrollment Report." www.grady.uga.edu/annualsurveys/Graduate_Survey/Graduate_2008/Grad2008Fullcolor.pdf.

45. As reported in "Median Age of Magazine Readers Rises," *Media Daily News*, May 26, 2009.

46. Bureau of Labor Statistics, *2010–2011 Occupational Outlook Handbook and Career Guide to Industries*.

47. Paul Farhi, "Men, Signing Off," *Washington Post*, July 23, 2006, citing a Radio and Television News Director Survey. www.washingtonpost.com/wp-dyn/content/article/2006/07/21/AR2006072100295.html. See also Collins, 353–354.

48. Bureau of Labor Statistics.

49. "Meet 25 Media Stars Who Moved from Old Media to New Media," *Business Insider*, April, 7 2010. www.businessinsider.com/meet-25-media-stars-who-leaped-from-old-media-to-new-media-2010-4.

50. Larissa A. Gruning, Linda Childers Hon, and Elizabeth A. Toth, *Women in Public Relations: How Gender Influences Practice* (New York: Guilford Press, 2001).

51. Ibid.

52. Bureau of Labor Statistics, "Meeting and Convention Planners."

53. "Women in Hospitality: Rich History, Bright Future, HCareers." See also Yan Zhon, *Factors Affecting Women's Career Opportunity in the Hospitality Industry* (PhD dissertation, Texas Tech University, 2006).

54. Deborah Tannen, *You Just Don't Understand* (New York: Ballantine Books, 1991); John Gray, *Men Are from Mars, Women Are from Venus* (New York: William Morrow, 1990).

55. For an affirmative answer, see Simon Baron-Cohen, *The Essential Difference* (New York: Basic Books, 2003).

56. John T. Cacioppo, Louis G. Tasinarry, and Gary G. Bernsten, *The Handbook of Psychophysiology* (Cambridge: Cambridge University Press, 2000), 541.

57. The debate goes on. For the argument for innate differences, in addition to Baron-Cohen above, see Steven Pinker, *The Blank Slate* (New York: Viking, 2002); or Luann Benzadine, *The Female Brain* (New York: Broadway Books, 2006) and *The Male Brain* (New York: Broadway Books, 2010). For a skeptical take, see Lise Eliot, *Pink Brain, Blue Brain* (New York: Houghton Mifflin Harcourt, 2009); Cordelia Fine, *Delusions*

of Gender (New York: Norton, 2010); and Elizabeth Spelke, "Sex Differences in Intrinsic Aptitude in Math and Science: A Critical Review," *American Psychologist* 5, no. 9 (December 2005): 950–958.

58. Brian Jacob, "Where the Boys Aren't," *Economics of Education Review* 21 (2002): 589–598. See also Gary S. Becker, William H. J. Hubbard, and Kevin M. Murphy, "The Market for College Graduates and the Worldwide Boom in Higher Education of Women," *American Economic Review* 100, no. 2 (May 2010): 229–233. http://mfi.uchicago .edu/programs/pdf/Becker%20Murphy%20Hubbard.pdf.

59. Lex Borghans, Bas Ter Weel, and Bruce A. Weinberg, "People People: Social Capital and the Labor Market Outcomes of Underrepresented Groups." *NBER Working Papers* 11985, National Bureau of Economic Research, 2006. See also Helen E. Fisher, *The First Sex: The Natural Talents of Women and How They Are Changing the World* (New York: Ballantine Books, 2000).

60. On this topic more generally, see Faith Popcorn, *Evolution: Eight Truths of Marketing to Women* (New York: Hyperion, 2000).

61. "Women in Marketing: Succeeding . . . Naturally!" Copernicus and Brandweek, 2006. www.copernicusmarketing.com/about/docs/women _success_in_marketing.pdf.

62. Claire Cain Miller, "Out of the Loop in Silicon Valley," *New York Times*, April 18, 2010.

63. Peter Coy, "The Slump: It's a Guy Thing," *Businessweek*, May 8, 2008.

64. See, for instance, Judith Rosener, *America's Competitive Secret: Using Women as a Management Strategy* (New York: Oxford University Press, 1995). Also see Alice H. Eagly and Linda L. Carli, "The Female Leadership Advantage: An Evaluation of the Evidence," *Leadership Quarterly* 14, no. 6 (December 2003): 807–834.

65. For a skeptical view of this "new feminism," see Schumpeter, "Womenomics," *The Economist*, December 30, 2009.

66. Margaret Mooney Marini et al., "Gender and Job Values," *Sociology of Education* 69, no. 1 (1996): 49–65. "Job Values" may help explain the exodus of women from the financial industry chronicled here: Kyle Stock, "The Ranks of Women on Wall Street Thin," *Wall Street Jour-*

nal, September 20, 2010. http://online.wsj.com/article/SB10001424
052748704858304575498071732136704.html?mod=googlenews_wsj.

67. Sylvia Ann Hewlett and Carolyn Buck Luce, "Off-Ramps and
On-Ramps: Keeping Talented Women on the Road to Success," *Harvard
Business Review*, March 2005. hbr.org/2005/03/on-ramps-and-off-ramps/
ar/1.

68. Quoted in Ruchika Tulshyan, "Top Ten College Majors for
Women," *Forbes*, March 2, 2010. www.forbes.com/2010/03/02/top-10
-college-majors-women-forbes-woman-leadership-education.html.

69. Heather Joslyn, "Women and Minorities Lag in Appointments to
Top Fundraising Jobs," *The Chronicle of Philanthropy*, September 6, 2010.
philanthropy.com/article/WomenMinorities-Lag-in/124249.

70. "2008 Grantmakers Salary and Benefits Report," Council on Federa-
tions. www.cof.org/files/Bamboo/programsandservices/research/documents/
08salarybenefitsexecsum.pdf.

71. Kindlon (see Introduction, note 11), 282.

72. Bureau of Labor Statistics, "The Employment Situation, August
2010," Table B-5. www.bls.gov/new.release/pdf/empsit.pdf.

73. AAUW, see Chapter 2, note 2.

74. "Women Lead in Doctorates," see Chapter 2, note 23.

75. See also this paper on the wage gap as a function of motherhood:
June O'Neill and Dave O'Neill, "What Do Wage Differentials Tell Us
About Labor Market Discrimination?" *Research in Labor Economics* 24
(2006): 293–357.

76. Betrand, Goldin, and Katz (see Chapter 2, note 30).

77. Diana Foster et al., "Off-Ramps and On-Ramps Revisited," New
York, Center for Work-Life Policy, June 1, 2010. Also in *Harvard Business Review*, June 2010.

78. According to the Census Bureau, in 2009 there were 158,000 married fathers taking care of their children full-time compared to 5.6 million
married mothers. "America's Families and Living Arrangements," March
2009, Current Population Survey. www.census.gov/newsroom/releases/
archives/families_households/cb10-08.html.

79. Kim Parker, "The Harried Life of the Working Mother," Pew Research Center, 2009.

80. See my "Femina Sapiens in the Nursery," *City Journal*, Autumn 2009. www.city-journal.org/2009/19_4_femina-sapiens.html.

81. Florida (see Chapter 1, note 11), 132. Also see my "Capitalists on Steroids," *City Journal*, Winter 2005. www.city-journal.org/html/15_1 _capitalists.html.

82. Goldin (see Introduction, note 8).

CHAPTER FOUR

1. John Hiscock, "This One's for the Kids," *The Telegraph*, December 11, 2008. www.telegraph.co.uk/culture/film/starsandstories/3709985/ Adam-Sandler-this-ones-for-the-kids.html.

2. U.S. Bureau of the Census, "Estimated Median Age at First Marriage." Table Ms-2. www.census.gov/population/socdemo/hh-fam/ms2.csv.

3. Pew Research Center, "The States of Marriage and Divorce," October 15, 2009. http://pewresearch.org/pubs/1380/marriage-and-divorce-by-state.

4. Frank F. Furstenburg Jr., "On a New Schedule: Transitions to Adulthood and Family Change," *The Future of Children* 20, no. 1 (Spring 2010): 71.

5. Reported in The Wooden Horse Publishing News Alert, August 15, 2002. www.woodenhorsepub.com/newsalerts/na8-15-02.htm.

6. "Average Total Paid and Verified Circulation for Top 100 ABC Magazines, 2009," Magazine Publishers of America. www.magazine.org/ CONSUMER_MARKETING/CIRC_TRENDS/ABC2009TOTAL rank.aspx. See also Stephanie Clifford, "Playboy Cuts Its Circulation," *New York Times*, October 20, 2009. http://mediadecoder.blogs.nytimes .com/2009/10/20/playboy-cuts-its-circulation/.

7. Numerous studies show that men don't read as many books as women, especially fiction. See, for instance, Harris Poll, March 2008, www.harrisinteractive.com/vault/Harris-Interactive-Poll-Research -Reading-2008-04.pdf; or "To Read or Not to Read: A Question of National Consequence," National Endowment of the Humanities, *Research Report* 47 (2007). www.nea.gov/research/toread.pdf.

8. Pew Project for Excellence in Journalism, "The State of the News Media: An Annual Report on American Journalism," 2010. www.state ofthemedia.org/2010/magazines_industry_overall.php.

9. Cover copy, Man Show, Season One. www.tvshowsondvd.com/reviews/Man-Season-One-Volume-1/2592.

10. Ellen McGirt, "How Adam Carolla Became a Podcast Superstar," *Fast Company*, April 1, 2010. www.adamcarolla.com/ACPBlog/press/fast-company/.

11. Bill Carter, "Home Base for Laughs? Comedy Central Thinks So," *New York Times*, March 28, 2007. www.nytimes.com/2007/03/28/arts/television/28come.html.

12. "Late Night Wars," TV by the Numbers, March 24, 2010. http://tvbythenumbers.com/2010/03/24/late-night-wars-stewie-pounds-leno-letterman-stewart-and-colbert-with-adults-18-34-adult-swim-wins-with-family-guy-reruns/45983.

13. Neil Genzlinger, "Damsels in Distress, Bozos in Heat," *New York Times*, January 29, 2010. www.nytimes.com/2010/01/31/arts/television/31sexes.html.

14. Entertainment Software Association, "Industry Facts," 2010. www.theesa.com/facts/index.asp.

15. Nielson Media, "The State of the Console," The Nielson Company, 2007. http://docs.google.com/viewer?a=v&q=cache:SmSrAP3yCYUJ:dataforbreakfast.com/wp-content/uploads/2007/08/nielsen_report_state_console_03507.pdf+nielson+media+%22state+of+the+console%22&hl=en&gl=us&pid=bl&srcid=ADGEESjFoXc1oRSNpa92U5o2uQu4QuVNL_4yQUvhgae9id7vURsBS0h72GH2C_-cCOonHXFOHHf8np20NAFeNA3oYX7RnvjTJSY7rz7-sfW040DKpBSb3-2rENSyEEbPsJxLb9_a0KfB&sig=AHIEtbTCovqxHjj-uh1g9SqvmPBhRPL1yA.

16. Leigh Alexander, "World of Warcraft Hits 10 Million Subscribers," *Gamasutra*, January 22, 2008. www.gamasutra.com/php-bin/news_index.php?story=17062.

17. "What Americans Do Online," Nielsonwire, August 2, 2010. http://blog.nielsen.com/nielsenwire/online_mobile/what-americans-do-online-social-media-and-games-dominate-activity/. For a broader discussion of the phenomenon, see Ethan Gilsdorf, *Fantasy Freaks and Gaming Geeks* (Guilford, DE: Lyons Press, 2009).

18. Maxim Overview, Demographics, 2002. Available at Google Documents: http://docs.google.com/viewer?a=v&q=cache:QX8oXnfE4

LQJ:www.ibiblio.org/pub/electronic-publications/stay-free/ml/
Maxim_2002.pdf+maxim+demographics&hl=en&gl=us&pid=bl&
srcid=ADGEESjiBPa4jPh9xV2hWUsSG8W.

19. See, for instance, Lyn Mikel Brown, Sharon Lamb, and Mark Tappan, *Packaging Boyhood: Saving Our Sons from Superheroes, Slackers, and Other Media Stereotypes* (New York: St. Martin's Press, 2009).

20. Nick Hornby, *About a Boy* (New York: Riverhead Trade, 1999), 7–8.

21. Susan Faludi, *Stiffed: The Betrayal of the American Man* (New York: William Morrow, 1999), 10. See also Michael Kimmel, *Manhood in America* (New York: Free Press, 1996); and R. W. Connell, *Masculinities* (New York: Blackwell, 2005).

22. Kimmel (see Introduction, notes 13,10, 45, 171). For a similar take, see Jessica Grose, "Omega Males and the Women Who Hate Them, " *Slate*, March 18, 2010. www.slate.com/id/2248156/.

23. Pew Research Center, "Millennials: Portrait of Generation Next," February 2010. http://pewsocialtrends.org/assets/pdf/millennials-confident -connected-open-to-change.pdf.

24. Donna L. Potts, "Channeling Girl Power," *Studies in Media and Information Literacy Education* 1, no. 4 (2001): 1–11.

25. Sandy Baum and Jessica Ma, "Education Pays: The Benefits of Higher Education for Individuals and Society," College Board, 2007. www.collegeboard.com/prod_downloads/about/news_info/cbsenior/yr2007/ ed-pays-2007.pdf.

26. Rachel Donadio, Sheelah Kolhatkar, and Anna Schneider-Mayerson, "Stuff-It, Emo-Boy," *New York Observer*, July 25, 2004. www .observer.com/2004/stuff-it-emo-boy.

27. Katie Roiphe, "The Naked and the Conflicted," *New York Times Book Review*, December 31, 2009. www.nytimes.com/2010/01/03/books/ review/Roiphe-t.html?pagewanted=3.

CHAPTER FIVE

1. David Gilmore, *Manhood in the Making* (New Haven: Yale University Press, 1990). Gilmore finds only two exceptions to the rule that men act as provider/protector—in Tahiti and Semai, both of them, he

notes, places unusually free of predators and enemies because "the harsher the environment and the scarcer the resources, the more manhood is stressed as inspiration and goal," 224. See also Gilbert H. Herdt, *Rituals of Manhood* (Berkeley: University of California Press, 1982).

2. Gilmore, 11.

3. Stephan M. Frank, *Life with Father: Parenthood and Masculinity in the Nineteenth Century American North* (Baltimore: Johns Hopkins University Press, 1998); Shawn Johansen, *Family Man: Middle Class Fatherhood in Early Industrializing America* (New York: Routledge, 2001).

4. John Tosh, *A Man's Place, Masculinity and the Middle Class Home in Victorian England* (Baltimore: Johns Hopkins University Press, 1998). See also Peter N. Stearns, *Be a Man: Males in Modern Society*, 2nd ed. (Teaneck, NJ: Holmes and Meier, 1990), Chapter 3.

5. Howard P. Chudacoff, *The Age of the Bachelor: Creating an American Subculture* (Princeton: Princeton University Press, 1999). See also David Nasaw, *Going Out: The Rise and Fall of Public Amusements* (New York: Basic Books, 1993).

6. Chudacoff.

7. Bill Ogersby, *Playboys in Paradise: Masculinity, Youth and Leisure Style in Modern America* (New York: Berg Publishers, 2001). See also John Strausbaugh, "Oh, Those Pulpy Days of 'Weasels Ripped My Flesh,'" Books of the Times, *New York Times*, December 9, 2004. www.nytimes.com/2004/12/09/books/09stra.html?_r=1&ex=1260334800&en=eae1982cadb6a578&ei=5090&partner=rssuserland.

8. Michael Kimmel, *Manhood in America: A Cultural History* (New York: Free Press, 1996), 82ff., 103.

9. Chudacoff, 230; E. Anthony Rotundo, *American Manhood* (New York: Basic Books, 1993), 248ff.

10. Eva Illouz, *Cold Intimacies: The Making of Emotional Capitalism* (Cambridge: Polity Press, 2007), 16.

11. See Kimmel and Rotundo, above. Also Gail Bederman, *Manliness and Civilization: A Cultural History of Gender and Race in the United States, 1880–1917* (Chicago: University of Chicago Press, 1995).

12. Tosh, 183. See also Judy Giles, *The Parlour and the Suburb: Domestic Identities, Class, Femininity, and Modernity* (New York: Berg Publishers, 2004).

NOTES

13. Rotundo, 254ff.

14. Sennett (see Chapter 1, note 58, 15). Faludi, see Chapter 4, note 21, puts it this way: the culture "defined manhood by the inner qualities of stoicism, integrity, reliability, the ability to shoulder burdens, the willingness to put others first, the desire to protect and provide and sacrifice," 38.

15. Quoted in Barbara Ehrenreich, *The Hearts of Men: American Dreams and the Flight from Commitment* (New York: Anchor Books, 1984), 48.

16. Ibid., 17.

17. It's sometimes forgotten how many of the most prominent second-wave feminists, usually following the theories of Friedrich Engels, rejected the institution of marriage—Simone de Beauvoir, Ti Grace Atkinson, Shulamaith Firestone, Germaine Greer, and Kate Millet; Betty Friedan, and Susan Brownmiller were exceptions.

18. One of the earliest voices was that of Carol Stack in *All Our Kin: Strategies for Survival in a Black Community* (New York: Basic Books, 1974). In the 1980s the television series *Murphy Brown* became a flashpoint on the topic. For more recent arguments on the subject, see Rosanna Hertz, *Single by Chance, Mothers by Choice* (New York: Oxford University Press, 2006); Jane Mattes, *Single Mothers by Choice: A Guidebook for Single Women Who Are Considering or Have Chosen Motherhood* (New York: Three Rivers Press, 1994); Peggy Drexler, *Raising Boys Without Men* (New York: Rodale Books, 2005); and Mikki Morrisette, *Choosing Single Motherhood: A Thinking Woman's Guide* (New York: Mariner Books, 2008).

19. Gary Cross, *Men to Boys: The Making of Modern Immaturity* (New York: Columbia University Press, 2008), 180.

20. Ibid., 41.

21. Neal Pollack, *Alternadad: The True Story of One Family's Struggle to Raise a Cool Kid in America* (New York: Random House, 2006), 221–222.

22. Kellie J. Hagewen and S. Philip Morgan, "Ideal and Intended Family Size in the United States: 1970–2002," *Population Development Review* 31, no. 3: 507–527. www.ncbi.nlm.nih.gov/pmc/articles/PMC2849141/. While the percentage of women who remain childless has in-

creased considerably (from 10 percent in 1985 to 18 percent in 2004), American women continue to cite two or three children as the ideal family size, as they have for many decades. Voluntary childlessness has been estimated to be about 7 percent in 2002. See Joyce C. Abma and Gladys M. Martinez, "Childlessness Among Older Women in the United States: Trends and Profiles," *Journal of Marriage and Family* 68, no. 4 (November 2006): 1045–1056. Catherine Hakim estimates voluntary childlessness in Europe at less than 10 percent. Catherine Hakim, "Childlessness in Europe," Research Report to Economic and Social Research Council, 2006. http://personal.lse.ac.uk/hakimc/_publications/ 2006_Childlessness_inEurope.pdf.

23. Eric D. Gould, "Marriage and Career: The Dynamic Decisions of Young Men," *Journal of Human Capital* 2, no. 4: 337–378. See also Hyunbae Chun and Injae Lee, "Why Do Married Men Earn More? Productivity or Marriage Selection?" *Economic Inquiry* 39, no. 2 (2001): 307–319; Matthias Pollman-Schult, "Marriage and Earnings: Why Do Married Men Earn More than Single Men?" *European Sociological Review*; Sanders Korenman and David Neumark, "Does Marriage Really Make Men More Productive?" *Journal of Human Resources* 26 (1990): 282–307.

24. Steven Nock, *Marriage in Men's Lives* (New York: Oxford University Press, 1998), Chapter 4.

25. Illouz.

26. Robert Weisman, "High Tech Falls for the Net," *Boston Globe*, April 8, 2009. www.boston.com/business/articles/2009/04/08/high_tech _falls_for_the_net/.

27. Ben Silverman, "World of Warcraft Astounding Numbers," Yahoo Games, September 18, 2010. http://videogames.yahoo.com/events/ plugged-in/world-of-warcraft-s-astounding-numbers/1355608.

28. Irin Carmon, "The Only Women in the Late Night Writers' Rooms," Jezebel.com, May 14, 2010. http://jezebel.com/5539213/the -only-women-in-the-late-night-writers-rooms?skyline=true&s=i.

29. Brewer's Association, Boulder, Colorado, "100 Year Brewery Count," www.brewersassociation.org/attachments/0000/0517/100-Years -HR.jpg.

CHAPTER SIX

1. Rosenfeld (see Chapter 1, note 2, Chapter 2).

2. Emily Flake, "Starving Artist," Sex and Dating Column, *Timeout New York* 513 (July 4, 2007). http://newyork.timeout.com/articles/sex -dating/8698/starving-artist.

3. Megan Carpentier, "There's Casual Sex, and Then There's Casual Sex." Jezebel.com, August 1, 2008. http://jezebel.com/5032110/theres-casual-sex-and-then-theres-casual-sex.

4. Annalee Newitz, "Cracking the Code to Romance," *Wired* 12, no. 6 (June 2004). www.wired.com/wired/archive/12.06/dating.html. The Soul Mate Manifesto can be accessed at www.solvedating.com/smintro.html.

5. Ellen K. Rothman, *Hands and Hearts: A History of Courtship in America* (Cambridge, MA: Harvard University Press, 1987); and Beth L. Bailey, *From Front Porch to Back Seat: Courtship in Twentieth Century America* (Baltimore: Johns Hopkins University Press, 1989).

6. Marguerite Fields, "Want to Be My Boyfriend? Please Define." Modern Love. Styles Section, *New York Times*, May 4, 2008. www.nytimes .com/2008/05/04/fashion/04love.html.

7. Julie Klausner, *I Don't Care About Your Band* (New York: Gotham, 2010), 150, 156.

8. Hannah Seligson, *A Little Bit Married: How to Know When It's Time to Walk Down the Aisle or Out the Door* (New York: Da Capo, 2009).

9. Quoted in Ibid., 77.

10. Michelle L. Devon, "One Night Stand Etiquette: The Polite Way of Going About a One-Night Stand," Your Tango, May 2, 2008. www .yourtango.com/20085221/one-night-stand-etiquette.

11. Jillian Strauss, *Unhooked Generation* (New York: Hyperion, 2003), 105.

12. John DeVore, "Mind of Man: Who Should Pay on the First Date?" The Frisky, May 14, 2009. www.thefrisky.com/post/246-mind-of-man -who-should-pay-for-the-first-date/.

13. Klausner, 229.

14. Anonymous, "The Man Shortage, Part Two," Spinbusters, October 22, 2009. Archived at http://web.archive.org/web/20091025211512/ geocities.com/remarksman/manshortage2.html.

15. Anonymous, "What Happened to All the Nice Guys?" Best of Craigslist LA, November 19, 2007. www.craigslist.org/about/best/lax/483 318927.html.

16. Johnny Diaz, "Tough Love," *Boston Globe*, June 20, 2006. www .boston.com/yourlife/articles/2006/06/20/tough_love/.

17. Mike Pilinski, "Alpha Male: How to Be a Nice Guy and Still Get Laid," Fastsecduction.com. http://www.fastseduction.com/alpha/001 -howtobeaniceguyandstillgetlaid.shtml.

18. Kevin Purcell, "How to Get Your Pickup Game Straight in Just One Weekend," *The Aquarian Weekly*, September 2006. For a history of, and some interesting observations about, Game, see also Charlotte Allen, "The New Dating Game," *Weekly Standard*, February 15, 2010.

19. Strauss, 47.

20. Toby Young, "So Did It Teach Us Anything Useful Along the Way?" *The Guardian*, May 11, 2008. www.guardian.co.uk/lifeandstyle/ 2008/may/11/women.film.

21. Whalen (see Chapter 1, note 66, 85).

22. Ibid., 80.

23. Pew Research Center, "The New Economics of Marriage: The Rise of Wives," January 19, 2010. http://pewresearch.org/pubs/1466/ economics-marriage-rise-of-wives?src=prc-latest&proj=peoplepress.

24. There is an average 2.7-year age gap preference between men and women, with the man older in each of thirty-five cultures. David M. Buss, "Sex Differences in Human Mate Preferences," *Behavioral and Brain Sciences* 12 (1989): 1–49.

25. Glinter J. Hitsch, Ali Hortacsu, and Dan Ariely, "What Makes You Click? An Empirical Analysis of Online Dating," UCSC Economics Department Seminars, October 1, 2004. http://escholarship.org/uc/ item/0410p1kq.

26. Gottlieb (see Chapter 2, note 79, 51).

27. Christian Rudder, "How Your Race Affects the Messages You Get," OK Trends, October 5, 2009. http://blog.okcupid.com/index.php/ your-race-affects-whether-people-write-you-back/. http://faculty.chicago booth.edu/emir.kamenica/documents/racialPreferences.pdf finds that women in general have stronger same-race preferences than men in speed dating.

28. "Bitter Asian Men," Yellowworld Forums. http://forums.yellowworld .org/showthread.php?t=25905.

29. Nikki Finke, "Terrifying TV, Showrunner Ed Bernero." Deadline Hollywood Daily, January 6, 2010. www.deadline.com/2010/01/terrifying -tv-showrunner-ed-bernero/.

30. Irina Aleksander, "Mad About the Man," *New York Observer*, October 14, 2008. www.observer.com/2008/arts-culture/mad-about-man ?page=0,1.

31. See this post by "Courtney A.," "I Slept with Tucker Max, the Internet's Biggest Asshat," Lemondrop.com, September 23, 2009. www.lemon drop.com/2009/09/23/i-slept-with-tucker-max-the-internets-biggest/.

32. "Reproductive Facts," American Society of Reproductive Medicine. www.reproductivefacts.org/uploadedFiles/ASRM_Content/Resources/ Patient_Resources/Fact_Sheets_and_Info_Booklets/agefertility.pdf.

33. Christian Rudder, "The Case for an Older Woman," OK Trends, February 16, 2010. http://blog.okcupid.com/index.php/2010/02/16/the-case-for-an-older-woman/.

34. Interview with the author, July 2008.

35. Rhoosh, "Solutions for Girls," RhooshV, May 9, 2007. http:// www.rooshv.com/solutions-for-girls/.

36. Nolan (see Introduction, note 1).

37. William Leith, "Revenge of the Geek," *The London Times*, February 15, 2008. www.timesonline.co.uk/tol/life_and_style/men/article337 0136.ece.

38. Sharon Lester, "One Big Problem with Dating in Your Thirties," Shine, Yahoo, July 8, 2010. http://shine.yahoo.com/channel/sex/one -big-problem-with-dating-in-your-thirties-1975976/.

39. Gottlieb, 75.

40. Jenny Blake, "Dating: Do You Go for Quantity or Quality?" Lifeaftercollege.com, August 26, 2009. www.lifeaftercollege.org/blog/ 2009/08/26/dating-quality-or-quantity/.

41. Amy Cohen, "Woo Is Me! The Courtship Question," *New York Observer*, May 6, 2001.

42. Strauss, 135.

43. Amy Cohen, "Daring to Date on an Island of Survivors," *New York Observer*, August 6, 2000.

44. Kate Harding, "Dating Don'ts: The Best Way Not to Get Laid," Salon.com, September 19, 2008. www.salon.com/life/broadsheet/2008/09/19/dating_donts/index.html.

45. Jill, "How Not to Get It On," Feministe.com, September 19, 2008. www.feministe.us/blog/archives/2008/09/19/how-not-to-get-it-on/.

46. Megan Carpentier, "A Guy's Guide to Not Getting It On," Jezebel .com, September 18, 2008. http://jezebel.com/5051963/a-guys-guide-to -not-getting-it-on.

CHAPTER SEVEN

1. Arthur C. Brooks, *Gross National Happiness* (New York: Basic Books, 2008), 64–70.

2. Roissy, "The Lie of Locking Her In," Citizen Renegade Blog, October 29, 2009. http://roissy.wordpress.com/2009/10/29/the-lie-of-locking -her-in/.

3. Bella DePaulo, *Singled Out* (New York: St. Martin's Griffin, 2007). See, among others, Barbara Feldon, *Living Alone and Loving It* (New York: Fireside, 2002); and Judy Ford, *Single: The Art of Being Satisfied, Fulfilled, and Independent* (Avon, MA: Adams Media, 2004).

4. U.S. Census Bureau, Facts for Features, July 19, 2010. www.census .gov/newsroom/releases/archives/facts_for_features_special_editions/cb1 0-ff18.html. Also, "We the People: Aging in the United States," Census 2000 Special Reports, December 2004.

5. Amy Cohen, *The Late Bloomer's Revolution: A Memoir* (New York: Hyperion, 2007), 92ff.

6. Rachel Lehman-Haupt, *In Her Own Sweet Time: Unexpected Adventures in Finding Love, Commitment and Motherhood* (New York: Basic Books, 2009), 32.

7. Sascha Rothchild, "How To Get Divorced by Thirty: A Beginners Guide to Ending Your Starter Marriage," *LA Weekly,* March 26, 2008. www.laweekly.com/2008-03-27/la-vida/how-to-get-divorced-by -30/. See also Rothchild's blog: http://sascharothchild.com/blog/category/ how-to-get-remarried-by-35/.

8. Andrew Cherlin, *The Marriage Go Round: The State of Marriage and the Family in America Today* (New York: Knopf, 2009), 28.

9. Betsey Stevenson, "Who's Getting Married? Education and Marriage Today," Council on Contemporary Families, January 26, 2010. www.contemporaryfamilies.org/images/stories/homepage/orange_border/ccf012510.pdf.

10. B. D. Whitehead and David Popenoe, "Changes in Teen Attitudes Towards Marriage, Cohabitation, and Children," The National Marriage Project, 1999. www.virginia.edu/marriageproject/pdfs/print_teenattitudes.pdf. The numbers from "Pathways to Adulthood and Marriage," an October 2008 study from the U.S. Department of Health and Human Services relying on four national surveys, are similar. http://aspe.hhs.gov/hsp/08/pathways2adulthood/rb.pdf.

11. Mindy E. Scott et al., "Young Adult Attitudes About Relationships and Marriage," Child Trends Research Brief, July 2009. www.childtrends.org/.../Child_Trends-2009_07_08_RB_YoungAdult Attitudes.pdf.

12. Richard A. Hessel and John H. Pryor, "Millennial Students," College Board National Forum, 2007. http://www.artsci.com/documents/CollegeBoardNatForumMillenialPresOct24_07.pdf. For a different set of findings, see "Coming of Age in America, Part II," Greenberg, Quinlon, Rosner Research, September 2005. www.greenbergresearch.com/articles/1010/2618_COA20905.pdf.

13. See Chapter 6, note 31.

14. Matthew D. Barmlett and William D. Mosher, "First Marriage, Divorce, Dissolution, and Remarriage," Advance Data Number 323, Center for Disease Control, May 31, 2001.

15. Norval Glenn, Jeremy Uecker, and Robert Love, "Later First Marriage and Marital Success," *Social Science Research*, September 2010: 787–800. The authors have found that while survival rates improve with later marriage, happiness levels do not.

16. Gretchen Livingston and D'Vera Cohn, "The New Demography of American Motherhood," Pew Research Center, August 19, 2010. http://pewsocialtrends.org/assets/pdf/754-new-demography-of-motherhood.pdf.

17. Madison Park and Miriam Falco, "Older Mothers' Kids Have Higher Rate of Autism, Study Finds," CNN.com, February 8, 2010.

http://articles.cnn.com/2010-02-08/health/autism.mother.age.risks
_1_autism-risk-autism-research-autism-rates?_s=PM:HEALTH.

18. Rebecca Smith, "IVF Children More Likely to Develop Cancer," *The Telegraph*, July 19, 2010. www.telegraph.co.uk/health/healthnews/7897088/IVF-children-more-likely-to-develop-cancer.html.

19. John Von Radoitz, "Birth Defects Caused by IVF Twice as Common, Study Finds," *Irish Examiner*, June 14, 2010. www.irishexaminer.com/world/health/birth-defects-caused-by-ivf-twice-as-common-study-finds-122378.html.

20. David Ellwood, "Fertility and Destiny," *Harvard Magazine*, March-April 2005. http://harvardmagazine.com/2005/03/fertility-and-destiny.html. As of this writing, the childless rate among all women in the United States is around 18 percent.

21. Phillip Longman, *The Empty Cradle: How Falling Birthrates Threaten World Prosperity and What to Do About It* (New York: Basic Books, 2004).

22. Rebecca Traister, "Attack of the Listless Lads," Salon, September 20, 2005. www.salon.com/books/int/2005/09/20/kunkel/print.html.

23. Jessica Salloway, "What's the Worst Nickname You Have for an Ex?" Lemondrop.com, October 6, 2009. www.lemondrop.com/2009/10/06/whats-the-worst-nickname-you-have-for-an-ex/.

24. Cohen (see Chapter 6, note 43).

25. Russ Ruggles, "Why You Should Lie in Your On-line Dating Profile," Online Dating Matchmaker, April 27, 21010. www.onlinedatingmatchmaker.com/lie-online-dating-profile/#more-457.

26. Lehman-Haupt, 22.

27. Neil Strauss, *The Game: Penetrating the Secret Society of Pickup Artists* (New York: IT Books, 2005), 183.

28. Norah Vincent. *Self-Made Man: One Woman's Journey into Manhood and Back* (New York: Viking, 2006).

29. Fields (see Chapter 6, note 6).

30. Stevenson. Less-educated men and women marry at noticeably lower rates; they also are more likely to have children when they are in their twenties and single.

31. One exception comes from Elizabeth Marquardt, Norval D. Glenn, and Karen Clark, "My Daddy's Name Is Donor: A New Study of Young

Adults Conceived by Sperm Donation," Commission on Parenthood's Future, Institute for American Values, 2010. http://familyscholars.org/my-daddys-name-is-donor-2/.

32. Christine Coppa, *Rattled: A Memoir* (New York: Broadway Books, 2009), 134.

33. Hertz (see Chapter 5, note 18).

34. Neilia Sherman, "On Your Own: Becoming a Single Mother by Choice," MomsToday.com, December 28, 2009. www.momstoday.com/articles/single-moms/on-your-own-2787/.

35. For a good summary of mainstream expert views on children and family structure from the Woodrow Wilson School of Princeton University and the Brookings Institution, see the issue devoted to the topic: "Marriage and Child Wellbeing," *The Future of Children* 15, no. 2 (Fall 2005).

36. Louise B. Silverstein and Carl F. Auerbach, "Deconstructing the Essential Father," *American Psychologist* 54, no. 6 (June 1999): 397–407.

37. Drexler (see Chapter 5, note 18).

38. Ehrenreich (see Chapter 5, note 15).

39. David Plotz, *The Genius Factory: The Curious History of the Nobel Sperm Bank* (New York: Random House, 2006), 192.

Acknowledgments

Once again, I find myself indebted to the William E. Simon Foundation. I'm deeply honored by their willingness to have me work under the title William E. Simon Fellow of the Manhattan Institute and infinitely grateful for the opportunity they've given me to pursue my interests. Heather Higgins and the Randolph Foundation have also been generous in their support.

For over a decade the Manhattan Institute has been my intellectual home; its influence will be apparent at many points in *Manning Up*. Special thanks to Larry Mone, Howard Husock, and Lindsay Young Craig, whose many years of backing and friendship have given me the freedom to ponder a wide range of themes, including some outside the usual ken of the Institute. Marcus Winters, Mark Riebling, Vanessa Mendoza, Clarice Smith, Kasia Zabawa, and George Ogden offered time and much appreciated support. Bernadette Serton was a source of useful advice and encouragement despite the demands of a new baby.

At *City Journal*, Brian Anderson oversaw the articles that served as the basis for *Manning Up* and encouraged their transformation into a book. Without his prodding, it's safe to say I would still be trying to figure out what to do next. I'm very grateful to have his cheerful and thoughtful guidance. Thanks to my *City*

Journal colleagues, especially Steve Malanga and Heather Mac Donald. Ben Plotinsky saved me from innumerable errors and embarrassments.

At Basic Books, Tim Sullivan was a wonderfully intelligent, pragmatic, though precipitously transplanted, editor. Thanks as well to Adam Khatib, Kärstin Painter, Lara Heimert, and Melissa Root.

Sheepish apologies go to my friends and family for having to put up with my obsessions and disappearances as deadlines loomed. Thankfully, they seemed to accept that a writer completing a book is by necessity, at least temporarily, a bad friend, sister, aunt, and cousin.

In all honesty, such a writer is not much of a wife or mother either. My husband, Paul, endured an emaciated social life and dinner conversation with few complaints. My children Dan, Nora, and most especially Anna, who was living at home as I completed *Manning Up*, also suffered my distractions with minimal eye-rolling. They did this knowing that the source of the distraction had the potential to embarrass them since, yet again, my subject matter was uncomfortably close to their own lives. I can't help it; their lives continue to interest me more than anything else.

Index